The Bible Speaks Today

Series Editors: J. A. Motyer (OT)
John R. W. Stott (NT)

The Message of Job
Suffering and grace

Titles in this series

The Message of Job

Suffering and grace

David Atkinson
Fellow and Chaplain, Corpus Christi College,
Oxford

Inter-Varsity Press
Leicester, England
Downers Grove, Illinois, USA

InterVarsity Press
38 De Montfort Street, Leicester LE1 7GP, England
P.O. Box 1400, Downers Grove, Illinois 60515, U.S.A.

InterVarsity Press®, USA, is the book-publishing division of InterVarsity Christian Fellowship®, a student movement active on campus at hundreds of universities, colleges and schools of nursing in the United States of America, and a member movement of the International Fellowship of Evangelical Students. For information about local and regional activities, write Public Relations Dept., InterVarsity Christian Fellowship, 6400 Schroeder Rd., P.O. Box 7895, Madison, WI 53707-7895.

Inter-Varsity Press, England, is the publishing division of the Universities and Colleges Christian Fellowship (formerly the Inter-Varsity Fellowship), a student movement linking Christian Unions in universities and colleges throughout the United Kingdom and the Republic of Ireland, and a member movement of the International Fellowship of Evangelical Students. For information about local and national activities in Great Britain write to UCCF, 38 De Montfort Street, Leicester LE1 7GP.

USA ISBN 0-8308-1230-X
USA ISBN 0-87784-925-0 (set of The Bible Speaks Today)
UK ISBN 0-85110-956-X

Phototypeset in Great Britain by Intype Ltd, London
Printed in the United States of America ∞

Library of Congress Cataloging-in-Publication Data
Atkinson, David John, 1943-
    The message of Job: suffering and grace/David Atkinson.
     p.   cm.—(The Bible speaks today)
    Includes bibliographical references.
    ISBN 0-8308-1230-X
    1. Bible. O.T. Job—Commentaries. I. Title. II. Series.
BS1415.3.A85 1992
223'.107—dc20   91-28680
                                      CIP

British Library Cataloguing in Publication Data
Atkinson, David, 1943-
  The message of Job: suffering and grace.—
  (The Bible speaks today)
  I. Title II. Series
  223.107

---

16 15 14 13 12 11 10 9 8 7 6 5 4 3
05 04 03 02 01 00 99

General preface

The Bible Speaks Today describes a series of both Old Testament and New Testament expositions, which are characterized by a threefold ideal: to expound the biblical text with accuracy, to relate it to contemporary life, and to be readable.

These books are, therefore, not 'commentaries', for the commentary seeks rather to elucidate the text than to apply it, and tends to be a work rather of reference than of literature. Nor, on the other hand, do they contain the kind of 'sermons' which attempt to be contemporary and readable without taking Scripture seriously enough.

The contributors to this series are all united in their convictions that God still speaks through what he has spoken, and that nothing is more necessary for the life, health and growth of Christians than that they should hear what the Spirit is saying to them through his ancient – yet ever modern – Word.

J. A. Motyer
J. R. W. Stott
Series Editors

For friends and colleagues
in the Oxford Christian Institute
for Counselling

Contents

Author's preface

These expository thoughts on the book of Job started life as a series of Bible readings given during morning worship in Wycliffe Hall Chapel, Oxford.

Job faces us with big questions: both personal and pastoral. The fact of suffering in the world touches us at many different levels. It may press on us most powerfully in the physical or emotional pain which we may have to endure. It may be our contact with others who are suffering, and the sense of helplessness we sometimes feel in the face of their distress. We may be more troubled at the intellectual level: why suffering? Can there be any point, any meaning in so much undeserved pain? Or it may touch us at the level of our relationship with God: where is God after the holocaust? What does my faith in God amount to in the light of my young next-door neighbour's inoperable cancer? Can we continue to speak of the love, care and compassion of God at times when all the evidence around us might suggest that he has let us down?

The book of Job is about all such questions. We meet a man who suffers physically and emotionally. We meet friends who do their best, but make things worse. We are brought face to face with the intellectual puzzles. And above and indeed because of all this, we find Job struggling with his faith in God.

In the end, we hear a word of divine grace. The justice, power and wisdom of God are proclaimed and vindicated. Job's pilgrimage ends in blessing. But there is a personal journey through many troubling chapters until we get there.

The book of Job has a power to reach into our human situation, and engage with our own needs. It tells it how it is. It is not comfortable reading. But because of its realism and its refusal to pretend that everything is all right when it feels all wrong, the book of Job does offer the strong sort of comfort which comes from our knowing that someone else has been there too.

The book of Job also raises pastoral questions. What could, or should, I be doing to help? What is appropriate care in a situation such as this? We will look back at Job from our Christian perspectives, from our side of the cross of Christ and of the empty tomb, with these pastoral concerns in front of us. What would Christian ministry require when faced with questions like these?

This book is less a commentary, more an exploration. I hope that it may be of use, especially to those involved in pastoral ministry, in helping us to bring our personal needs and questions into the light of the Wisdom of God which shines through even the dark pages of Job.

I have based my exposition on the New International Version of the Bible, but sometimes I have also used my own paraphrases.

For some years I have been secretary to the Council of Management of the Oxford Christian Institute for Counselling. This is a charitable trust which seeks to supplement and co-operate with the pastoral care of local churches in the Oxford area by offering a service of counselling, support and training. Many Jobs have sought help from OCIC's staff; many have found relief and support from OCIC's Christian care. In honour of OCIC's desire to offer a counselling service in a Christian context, I dedicate this book to them.

Bibliography

F. I. Andersen, *Job* (*Tyndale Old Testament Commentary*, IVP, 1976).

O. Chambers, *Baffled to Fight Better: Talks on the Book of Job* (Marshall, Morgan & Scott, 1931).

D. A. Clines, *Job 1 – 20* (Word Books, 1989).

S. R. Driver, *The Book of Job in the Revised Version* (Clarendon, 1906).

R. Gordis, *The Book of God and Man: A Study of Job* (University of Chicago Press, 1965).

N. C. Habel, *The Book of Job* (SCM Press, 1985).

A. and M. Hanson, *The Book of Job* (*Torch Bible Commentaries*, SCM Press, 1953).

J. E. Hartley, *The Book of Job* (Eerdmans, 1988).

E. W. Heaton, *The Hebrew Kingdoms* (OUP, 1968).

E. Jones, *The Triumph of Job* (SCM Press, 1966).

A. S. Peake, *Job* (*Century Bible*, T. C. & E. C. Jack, 1905).

M. H. Pope, *Job* (Doubleday, 1965).

H. H. Rowley, *From Moses to Qumran* (Lutterworth, 1963).

H. H. Rowley, *Job* (Nelson, 1970).

N. H. Snaith, *The Book of Job* (SCM Press, 1968).

S. Terrien, 'Job', in *The Interpreter's Bible*, vol. 3 (Abingdon Press, 1954).

J. Wood, *Job and the Human Situation* (Bles, 1966).

1. Righteous Job and the wager in heaven
(Job 1 – 3)

Any answers?

The church notice-board carried the announcement, 'Christ is the answer'. Someone had written next to it, 'Yes, but what is the question?' And what if looking for answers is not always appropriate, in any case?

Much of our modern world is concerned with finding answers. Our technological mentality sees the world as something we can understand and control. We tend to see life in terms of questions which need answering, in terms of problems which need solving; in terms of causes and effects.

In his marvellous little book *The Other Side of 1984*, Bishop Lesslie Newbigin explores these aspects of contemporary culture. He writes:

> As heirs of the Englightenment and representatives of the 'modern scientific world view', our normal procedure is to list a series of 'problems', identify their causes, and then propose 'solutions' based on a scientific analysis of the situation. We normally proceed on the assumption that there must in principle be a solution which proper research can identify and proper techniques can deliver.[1]

But he rightly goes on to dispute this common view. He continues:

[1] L. Newbigin, *The Other Side of 1984* (World Council of Churches, 1983), pp. 18–19.

Today we are becoming sceptical about this approach. We are coming to see that there are 'problems' in human life for which there are no 'solutions'. The question has to be asked whether we do not need new models for understanding our human situation.[2]

The truth is that it is often important not to answer the question; it is sometimes important to fail and to fall. When commenting in 1983 on the proposals of the then Secretary of State for Education, Sir Keith Joseph, to give all school-leavers a 'certificate of character', Bishop John V. Taylor wondered whether the intended certificate could be drawn in such way as to invite the statement, 'This pupil knows how to fail.' He continued:

> Yet that is a very rare and much needed form of strength. Three years ago, I said to the daughter of some friends of ours, a brilliant girl who had just won her scholarship to the university: 'One of these days you will taste failure, and I don't know how you are going to cope with it.'[3]

God sometimes allows or, dare we say, ordains that we walk in the valley of the shadow, perhaps because it may be that there is no other way of discovering the power of his comforting rod and staff. Or perhaps it is because of some inscrutable providence of his own in which – in all his love and grace, and not in the slightest manipulatively – he calls on us to be his servants through our pains and our frailties within wider purposes in heaven than we on earth can discern.

This seems to be part of the point of the book of Job. There are, we shall see, many problems and many questions. But there is precious little that will count in the way of an 'answer' as we usually understand that term. We are face to face with a good and godly man who suffers – suffers intolerably and seemingly endlessly. He catches us up into his pain, into his misery, into the injustice of it all. He envelops us in his plea to God to tell him what on earth, or what in hell, is going on. He covers us with his sense of abandonment – by family, by friends, by God himself. And there is *nothing* that we can say to ease his plight; there is *nothing* we can do which makes things any better.

Journey to the edge
The book of Job brings us to the edge. It confronts us with failure,

---

[2] *Ibid.*, p. 19.
[3] Bishop John V. Taylor, in the Hockerkill Foundation Lecture, 1983.

and with suffering for which there is no explanation. It faces us with the inadequacy of ministry; with the inappropriateness of some forms of preaching; with a God who seems silent, callous, unfair and remote. We are forced to rethink our prejudices; rethink our theology; rethink the meaning of pastoral care in the face of injustice and suffering; rethink what we say about God. And though at the end of the day, the book brings us back to the all-sufficiency of divine grace, and stands out amongst the Wisdom literature in the Bible as a plea to see things from a divine and not a human perspective, there is a long, painful and arduous path to climb before we hear the Lord speaking, as he does at the end of the book, from the whirlwind.

Innocent suffering

The major theme of the inscrutable mystery of innocent suffering is one which all of us who are not blind to the world in which we live, or whose heads are not blissfully buried in the sand, have to encounter. It is not only the horrors of the holocaust which pro-voke the searching questions for believers in God: Why did God allow this? Where was God in all this? Can there even be belief in God after Auschwitz? The question presses on us also in the abuse by which some children's lives are blighted; in the hurricane which sweeps away a house and a family within it; in an earthquake which takes the lives of thousands; or in the death of the innocent through a terrorist bomb. In some of these we may see the hand of sinful men and women, and perhaps blame them for the innocent suffer-ing they have caused. In others, we can see only the hand of God. Are we then to blame him? And why does God seems so capricious in his care? Why will he heal one person's illness, but not another's? Why be concerned with one person's illness in any case, when he seems inactive in the face of the deaths of millions in a gas chamber? These are questions we have all asked. The book of Job will not give us easy answers. But it will open up for us ways into the struggle for women and men of faith. It will show us how one man at the end of the day was enabled by grace to live with his questions.

As we explore these chapters, may we find growing within us a deeper sensitivity to the human situation. We need to be prepared to be confronted, as Job's friends were, with the horror of some human pain. We may need to let our defences down in a way that his friends found hard to do, and allow ourselves to hear Job questioning God, despairing at the way God runs the world. May God help us stick with it in a way that his friends could not. They could not live with the human suffering which Job embodied. They had to look for causes. They wanted solutions. They had to search for answers. They were uncomfortable when face to face with that which defied the logic of their own theological position. They had to proclaim the truth. They insisted on treating suffering only as a problem to be solved, rather than being willing to cope with the uncertainty of facing its mystery. And they received a pretty sharp word from the Lord at the end of the day for doing so (see 42:7). This book asks us to walk *with* Job right through the depths of his struggle, open to wherever he takes us, for only so will we catch the significance of the Lord's gracious voice at the story's end.

The pattern of the book

But this is to move ahead. We need to begin at the beginning.

The book of Job falls into three clear sections. It starts (chapters 1 and 2) with a prose prologue in which the scene is set, and in which earthly and heavenly realities are placed side by side. Matching this, the book ends with a prose epilogue (42:7–14) which serves a particular purpose at the end of the story, and brings the book to its conclusion. In between there is the body of the book which is a long poem (3:1 – 42:6) in which Job and his friends try to argue out the situation, and in which eventually Job hears the voice of God.

Some commentators believe that the real story begins in chapter 3, and they understand chapters 1 and 2 as a later addition. However, as we shall see, these chapters are integral to the story, and set the context in which the reader is atuned to the themes which follow in the rest of the book.

We do not know who wrote the book of Job, nor anything about the author beyond what we can glean from the text. Neither do we know when the book was written, though it is possible that an ancient folk tale was picked up and woven into this masterly epic poem. A recognized tradition about Job is referred to in Ezekiel 14:14. What is clear is that our author is a master story-teller. The prologue, chapters 1 and 2, is essential to his plot.

So we begin with Job chapters 1 and 2, the story of the heavenly wager.

1. Behind the scenes in the heavenly court (1:1 – 2:8)

In the land of Uz there lived a man whose name was Job. This man was blameless and upright; he feared God and shunned evil. *²He had seven sons and three daughters, ³and he owned seven thousand sheep, three thousand camels, five hundred yoke of oxen* and five hundred donkeys, and had a large number of servants. He was the greatest man among all the people of the East.

⁴His sons used to take turns holding feasts in their homes, and they would invite their three sisters to eat and drink with them. ⁵When a period of feasting had run its course, Job would send and have them purified. Early in the morning he would sacrifice a burnt offering for each of them, thinking, 'Perhaps my children have sinned and cursed God in their hearts.' This was Job's regular custom.

⁶One day the angels came to present themselves before the LORD, and Satan also came with them. ⁷The LORD said to Satan, 'Where have you come from?'

Satan answered the LORD, 'From roaming through the earth and going to and fro in it.'

⁸Then the LORD said to Satan, 'Have you considered my servant Job? There is no-one on earth like him; he is blameless and upright, a man who fears God and shuns evil.'

⁹'Does Job fear God for nothing?' Satan replied. ¹⁰'Have you not put a hedge around him and his household and everything he has? You have blessed the work of his hands, so that his flocks and herds are spread throughout the land. ¹¹But stretch out your hand and strike everything he has, and he will surely curse you to your face.'

¹²The LORD said to Satan, 'Very well, then, everything he has is in your hands, but on the man himself do not lay a finger.'

Then Satan went out from the presence of the LORD.

¹³One day when Job's sons and daughters were feasting and drinking wine at the oldest brother's house, ¹⁴a messenger came to Job and said, 'The oxen were ploughing and the donkeys were grazing nearby, ¹⁵and the Sabeans attacked and carried them off. They put the servants to the sword, and I am the only one who has escaped to tell you!'

¹⁶While he was still speaking, another messenger came and said, 'The fire of God fell from the sky and burned up the sheep and the servants, and I am the only one who has escaped to tell you!'

¹⁷While he was still speaking, another messenger came and said, 'The Chaldeans formed three raiding parties and swept down on your camels and carried them off. They put the servants to the sword, and I am the only one who has escaped to tell you!'

¹⁸While he was still speaking, yet another messenger came and said, 'Your sons and daughters were feasting and drinking wine at the oldest brother's house, ¹⁹when suddenly a mighty wind swept in from the desert and struck the four corners of the house. It collapsed on them and they are dead, and I am the only one who has escaped to tell you!'

²⁰*At this, Job got up and tore his robe and shaved his head. Then he fell to the ground in worship* ²¹*and said:*

> *Naked I came from my mother's womb,*
>   *and naked I shall depart.*
> *The LORD gave and the LORD has taken away;*
>   *may the name of the LORD be praised.'*

²²*In all this, Job did not sin by charging God with wrongdoing.*

²:¹*On another day the angels came to present themselves before the LORD and Satan also came with them to present himself before him.* ²*And the LORD said to Satan, 'Where have you come from?'*

Satan answered the LORD, 'From roaming through the earth and going to and fro in it.'

³*Then the LORD said to Satan, 'Have you considered my servant Job? There is no-one on earth like him; he is blameless and upright, a man who fears God and shuns evil. And he still maintains his integrity, though you incited me against him to ruin him without any reason.'*

⁴*"Skin for skin!" Satan replied. 'A man will give all he has for his own life.* ⁵*But stretch out your hand and strike his flesh and bones, and he will surely curse you to your face.'*

⁶*The LORD said to Satan, 'Very well, then, he is in your hands; but you must spare his life.'*

⁷*So Satan went out from the presence of the LORD and afflicted Job with painful sores from the soles of his feet to the top of his head.* ⁸*Then Job took a piece of broken pottery and scraped himself with it as he sat among the ashes.*

The first and most important thing we are to notice about chapters 1 and 2 is the literary device our author uses to tell us what is going on: two stories are woven together, one taking place in heaven, the other on earth.

The man from Uz

We begin on earth (1:1–5) and in the land of Uz (wherever that may be), and we learn that Job, the central character in the story, was a rich man with seven sons and three daughters, numbers which signify completeness. He was a man in his middle years with a grown family, but still young enough to father ten further children – as we learn at the end of the book (42:13). He was 'blameless and upright' (1:1), a good man. He could not be charged with wrong before God or man. He was pious and moral, 'a man who fears God and shuns evil' (1:1, 8; 2:3). He was internationally known as a person of considerable substance. Job 1:3 tells us that he was the greatest man of all the people of the East.

Material prosperity

It is important for us to remember that in the Hebrew culture material prosperity was often understood as a sign of God's blessing. Deuteronomy 28 indicates as much, in its antithesis between the blessings which will come to the person who obeys God, and the cursings which are the consequences of disobedience. In fact, there is much in the Bible which supports the view of the psalmist in Psalm 1:

> Blessed is the man
>> who does not walk in the counsel of the wicked . . .
> The LORD watches over the way of the righteous,
>> but the way of the wicked will perish.[4]

God is a good creator, concerned for the well-being of his world. The people of God can trust him for their welfare, and leave their well-being in his hands. This is a moral universe in which virtue is rewarded, and in which evil is punished. God is again and again presented in the Bible as a God who is good, and who rewards those who diligently seek him,[5] who live obediently in fellowship with him. Material well-being is sometimes part of the way God shows his blessing.

This is by no means the whole story, however. For alongside the faith of Psalm 1 we need also to remember, for example, the faith of Psalm 42 in which the psalmist is downcast at his predicament, and of Psalm 73 in which the psalmist is dismayed by his misfortunes and the contrasting prosperity of the wicked. Life in God's world is by no means always marked by material prosperity here and now. Though we may believe that God knows what is for our good, it is by no means clear that this will always be obvious to us. There is a dark side, in other words, to living in God's world. Sometimes we are under God's shadow. There are aspects of God's dealings with us which do not seem on the face of it to be much to do with our well-being at all. There is a struggle of faith, as well as a contentment in God's provision. It is this dark side which, we shall see, the book of Job so vividly portrays.

A good man

Job was a good and godly man – everyone could see that. Our

[4] Ps. 1:1, 6.   [5] Cf. Heb. 11:6.

author wants us to be in no doubt about this. A more caring, upright, godly and good person it is hard to imagine. This makes all the more poignant the contrast with the mishaps which are about to befall him.

Job's piety and care extended to offering sacrifices as the priest of the family on behalf of his children (1:5). He wanted his family to be purified from sin. 'Perhaps my children have sinned and cursed God in their hearts,' he wondered (1:5). To curse God, Job knew, was sin, and he wanted his whole family to be kept clean. So he would rise early in the morning (a Hebrew idiom for 'conscientiously'), and offer burnt offerings. This was his life-long habit, his 'regular custom' (1:5).

The heavenly court

Then in verse 6 the scene changes. We are suddenly reminded that there are more things in heaven and earth than are dreamed of in many philosophies. We recall that, as we learn in Genesis 1, the Lord is Creator of 'the heavens and the earth'. And 'heaven', of course, stands for that part of God's created order which is his dwelling place; the location of his heavenly court.

Job 1 does not use the word 'heaven', but it refers to 'the presence of the LORD' (1:12) to mean exactly this. There is another realm, another place, where God holds council with his heavenly court and where actions are taken which affect people on earth. Job does not see this. There is no indication that he is ever aware of it. In fact, it is centrally important to the story that he is completely unaware of this whole dimension to his predicament. All Job knows is the suffering which results. But we, the readers, are told. We are given a glimpse of the heavenly realm of which Job himself remains ignorant.

The Satan

The courtiers were there. So was the court 'Adversary', the one whose task it was to make out a case for the opposition: Satan, the prosecuting angel, an 'official of the secret police'.[6] We must beware of reading back too much of the New Testament understanding of the devil into this figure of the Satan. The satanic being's identity was gradually pictured in ever clearer and more evil terms until by the time we reach the Gospels, 'Satan' is the name given to the devil. But here he is 'the Adversary' who has been going to and fro on the earth to test the characters of God's people, trying, it seems, to find evidence of disloyalty among the people of God.

[6] Jones, p. 27.

And not only so, he appears to delight in it. The picture given here is of a being who seems wholly committed to the downfall of righteous and godly people.

So the Satan comes into court, where God asks what he has been up to. Then God initiates the drama of the book of Job by drawing attention to Job's character. 'Have you considered my servant Job?' (1:8). (Notice, in passing, this reference to Job as God's 'servant'. The significance of this will become clearer later on.)

The Satan's taunt

But the Satan, whose preoccupation with hunting out wrongdoing has produced a cynicism which is destructive, replies to God in effect, 'Do you think Job's piety is all for nothing? You don't think he does all this without expecting some reward, do you? In any case, he is a bad example of piety – you, God, have hedged him in with so much wealth, richness, and family support (1:10). No wonder he is good! In the real world of pain, of bereavement, of struggle, people are not good. Take away Job's possessions and he will fail – he will curse you to your face. Goodness cannot survive in the real world of human pain.'

This is the Satan's taunt. This question becomes one of the central issues of the rest of the book: 'Does Job fear God for nothing?' (1:9). In other words: can there be such a thing as disinterested goodness? Is Job only good because of what he can get out of it? The question sometimes comes to us like that also: 'Are people only religious because of what they can get out of it? Is your faith in God dependent only on the good you think it will do you?'

Some psychologists of religion distinguish what they call 'extrinsic' religion from what they call 'intrinsic' religion. A person's religion is said to be 'extrinsic' if he *uses* it for some other purpose. Perhaps religion is for such a person a social status symbol, or a set of rituals for alleviating anxiety. By 'intrinsic' religion, these psychologists mean that a person does not so much *use*, as *live* his or her faith. The distinction can be expressed by saying that for some people their faith in God serves as a means to some other end, whereas for others, God is seen as an end in himself. This question at the centre of the book of Job is addressed to us all. Why do we serve God? Is it just for what we can get out of it? Or is ours a faith rooted in the reality of a personal communion with God himself – for his sake?

Does Job serve God for nothing?

Satan says, 'No.' The accusing Satan suggests that Job serves God, and worships him, only because of the material prosperity he will gain. In saying this, he puts his own explanation and interpretation of Job's behaviour against God's view, and in doing so, of course, shows that he has no understanding of the reality of Job's true relationship with God as one of inner communion. Satan suggests that Job's relationship with God is merely one of a contract which has benefits both for Job in terms of his prosperity, and for God in terms of his illusory belief that he has evoked a real response from Job.[7] Satan misses the fact that the really important thing for Job is that he *lives*, not merely *uses*, his faith. His communion with God is all important. As we shall see towards the end of the book, it is the reality of personal communion with God which eventually rescues Job from his predicament.

The Satan on a chain

God's reply is to give Satan the freedom to try Job out. God sets the bounds. There is evil here, but not dualism, and perhaps we need to pause to register that fact. A great deal of popular Christian thinking operates with a sort of dualism, in which the whole of life is understood in terms of a battle between God and Satan, or between the Holy Spirit and the world of the demonic, as though these were all equal partners in a contest. Of course it is sometimes easier to interpret our lives in terms of a conflict between heavenly powers than to take appropriate responsibility ourselves. But a dualism of good and evil is not the teaching of the Bible. While we must not ignore the reality of spiritual warfare, we must remember that the contest is not between equals. There is no equal and opposite force of evil in tension with the goodness of God. Such a view is not found in the Bible. Rather, God is always sovereign. And Satan is always only an adversary on a chain. Satan is always under God's authority and control. It is the sovereign God who says, 'Everything he has is in your hands, but on the man himself do not lay a finger' (1:12). So Satan, we are told, went out from the presence of the Lord.

Back on earth

In verse 13, the scene changes back to earth where, all unaware of the conversation in heaven, Job's sons and daughters were feasting as, it seems, was their fairly regular custom. They used to take turns in holding feasts in their homes (1:4). Job's experience on earth was in the here and now; its full significance was elsewhere. All unknowingly, Job has become involved in a demonstration in heaven of how God rules his world. *God* is using Job as his

---

[7] *Cf.* Jones, p. 28.

suffering servant for heavenly purposes of his own. Job's own soul has become caught up in the strategies of heaven.

The family were in the eldest brother's house, which means it was the beginning of the week. It also means that Job had just offered a burnt offering sacrifice on their behalf. The author wants us to be absolutely sure that there was no secret sin lurking in Job or his family. All had just been made clean. Neither Job nor his family were sinless, but Job was genuinely good. He was in the right before God. There were no outstanding issues between God and Job, or between God and Job's family, awaiting settlement. The sacrifice had been made.

Disaster

And then, into this goodness, comes stab after stab of the dagger of misfortune: four messengers run to Job one after the other (see 1:14–19):

'The Sabeans have taken your herds and killed your servants; I alone have escaped to tell you.'

'A crack of lightning has struck your flock of sheep and the shepherds; I alone have escaped to tell you.'

'The Chaldeans have raided your camels and killed those servants too, and I alone have escaped to tell you.'

'A cyclone has struck the house where all your children were feasting – they are all dead. I alone have escaped to tell you.'

What power there is in this passage! If Shakespeare had dramatized this, what a play we would have had!

Worship

But the Satan was proved wrong. Job did not curse God. He did not go hunting around for secondary causes. He did not search for anyone to blame. He took it all as from the hand of God. And he *worshipped*. In a verse of great dignity, we read. 'At this, Job got up and tore his robe and shaved his head. Then he fell to the ground in worship and said: "Naked I came from my mother's womb, and naked I shall depart. The LORD gave and the LORD has taken away; may the name of the LORD be praised" ' (1:20–21).

Even in all this Job sees the hand of God. Amazingly, and significantly, his first instinct is to react Godwards – in worship. How few of us find that worship is our first reaction even at the best of times. But here is a man who is coping with a multiple bereavement. He has been afflicted with loss after loss. His sorrow is real and very great. How difficult it is to worship at such a time! Yet worship is Job's reaction. He is so absorbed by the sovereign action of God in giving and in taking away that there is a humble acceptance in blessing even the hand that has struck him. Would that we could learn to make that our first reaction to crisis – to pray. How important in pastoral ministry to seek to lead others who are in pain to place their needs before God.

Back in heaven

The scene now changes once again and reverts to the heavenly court. Job 2 opens with another occasion when the angels come to present themselves before the Lord, Satan also with them once more. Again the little ritual is enacted, God asking Satan what he has been up to, and Satan replying. Then, once again, the Lord asks Satan whether he has considered Job. 'He is blameless and upright, a man who fears God and shuns evil. And he still maintains his integrity, though you incited me against him to ruin him without any reason' (2:3). The picture is almost identical with that of chapter 1, but with three additions. Satan not only comes with the other angels, but actually presents himself before the Lord (2:1). Is this to acknowledge that God won the first round of the contest, and Satan, perhaps mockingly, bows in obeisance? Then, secondly, God adds to his words that Job 'maintains his integrity' (2:3), underlining Job's righteous character. And thirdly , God adds, 'You incited me against him to ruin him.' The sentence probably then should continue, 'but all for nothing!' (2:3). All the Satan's taunts have come to nothing so far. God chides the Satan: Job did not lose his integrity! To which Satan replies (2:4) 'Skin for skin!' This is a very difficult verse to understand, but possibly means: 'What we have done so far is just skin deep; we have only scratched the surface. Touch his own life – his flesh and bones, and he will surely curse you to your face' (2:5).

So, for reasons which are not clear to us – let alone to Job, who of course is totally unaware of the heavenly issue involved – God sets the further bounds of Satan's activities, and gives him permission for this further test. Sickness is added to all the other trials Job has to face. With God's permission, Job is afflicted by Satan with this intolerably loathsome condition. The painful sores (2:7) from the soles of his feet to the top of his head are variously described as a sort of leprosy or elephantiasis. He takes himself out to where the lepers go: the ash heap outside the city, where he scrapes at his sores with a piece of broken pottery. He who was rich now becomes poor. God's servant suffers.

2. The suffering of faith

Satan's jibes have proved false. 'A man's life does not consist in the abundance of his possessions.'[8] God's trust in Job has been vindicated. Job does not curse God. He retains his faith. But that now becomes his biggest problem of all!

The author has skilfully brought us face to face with the unchanging human perils of war, destitution, sickness, humiliation, bereavement and depression. War is mentioned in the attack of the Sabeans in 1:15; destitution in the loss of Job's sheep and camels in 1:16–17. Job's humiliation is implicit in the change depicted from the man of wealth to the man sitting on the ash heap scraping his sores. His sickness is the covering of his body from head to toe with loathsome boils (2:7). Job is bereaved in the loss of all his children in 1:19, and as we shall see in chapter 3, depression is just round the corner.

God's hidden hand

The hand of God is hidden. We, from outside the story, can distinguish God's permissive will from his perfect ordering of the world, and of course we need to. We cannot simply accept disaster as God's appointment, as part of his design for the world. His perfect order is: no sin, no sickness, no satanic tests. But this world is not as God originally made it, pronouncing it 'good'. At point after point in God's world, the structured harmonies of God's good creation have become discordant and harsh. This world is an ambiguous 'fallen' world, now marked not only by the beauties of creation, but also by disorder, pain, struggle and death.

The distinction between God's perfect will and his permissive will needs to be made. It is clearly seen, for example, in the biblical story of Noah. After the Flood, God again says to Noah what he said at the start of creation: 'Be fruitful and multiply',[9] but the tone now is different. God speaks of fear and dread, and he gives laws to curb human sinfulness. This is no longer the Garden of Eden. The world this side of the Fall is a broken world, and though God's will is still made clear to us, it comes refracted through the needs of a fallen world. The first two chapters of the book of Job have indicated the divine *permission* to the Satan to afflict Job. We cannot read that as God's perfect will as though we were still in the Garden of Eden. We can distinguish God's perfect will from his permission. But Job cannot at this point see enough to make that distinction.

[8] Lk. 12:15.   [9] Gn. 9:1–17.

Bewilderment . . .

From Job's perspective it is simply bewildering. Satan's involvement is not suspected at all. It all seems so natural: terrorists, lightning, a cyclone; things like this happen to people, as we know from our newspapers all too well. In this sense, Job is Everyman: his needs are human needs. But in another sense Job was out on his own. He was a righteous and godly man, a paradigm of goodness. He was the most extreme example of bad things happening to good people. Yet Job insists on seeing his misfortune as the hidden hand of God.

And that is his problem!

Now the real major burden of the book of Job begins to unfold. Job's faith does not relieve his suffering, it makes it worse. To some extent it causes it.

Job's faith was based on the living God who cares for his people. It was faith in Yahweh, the Covenant Lord, the God of justice, mercy and goodness. Job knows God's grace (why else would he offer burnt offerings?). For him, God in grace prospered the upright man; God, thought Job, blesses the righteous. Now, however, Job has to square this faith with his own desperate situation. Everything Job believed about God was being called in question.

. . . and faith

It is important to remember that this question of human suffering could be asked in the way it is in the book of Job only *because of* Job's (and the author's) fundamental commitment of faith. Suffering, in fact, is only a *problem* to the person with faith in a good God. The atheist, of course, has to come to terms with suffering, but for him it is merely a fact, part of the absurdity, perhaps, of the world. But the fact that many people perceive suffering to be a *problem* is itself a witness to the fact that there exists a good God, in whose light the existence of suffering poses us questions. As Francis I. Andersen comments:

> There are no 'accidents' in a universe ruled by the one sovereign Lord. Hence Job's problem. Such mishaps are not a problem for the polytheist, the dualist, the atheist, the naturalist, the fatalist, the materialist, the agnostic. An annoyance, a tragedy even, but not a problem. Suffering caused by human wickedness or by the forces of nature is ultimately a problem only for a believer in the one Creator who is both good and almighty; so this problem

JOB 1 - 3

can only arise within the Bible with its distinctive moral mono-
theism.[10]

So has God done something bad? Whence these inexplicable
providences? Where is God's justice? What is God doing in all
this? What comfort can faith offer now?

Uncertainties

In *A Grief Observed*, C. S. Lewis, struggling agonizingly with God
(whom at one point he calls 'the Cosmic Sadist') in the face of the
death of his wife, says, 'Talk to me about the truth of religion and
I'll listen gladly. Talk to me about the duty of religion and I'll
listen submissively. But don't come talking to me about the consolations of religion, or I shall suspect that you don't understand.'[11]
We the readers have been let into a little of the secret behind the
scenes in the heavenly court. But there is much we do not understand. That is true for Christian faith also. Even though God has
disclosed to us much more of his purposes in Christ than Job could
even dream of, there is a hidden world of divine purposes of which
we know only a part. For us, too, 'the secret things belong to the
LORD our God.'[12] Faith is learning to trust God in the dark, in
unknowing, in apparent failure. Faith is what God gives us to help
us live with uncertainties.
We can only watch in anguish as Job and those near him, who
have nothing to go on but their faith and their experience, struggle
with the question of how to keep faith and experience together. The
great onslaught of destruction paralyses all platitudes and forces us
to the edge of meaning. Are we willing to come and stand there
with Job, and with all the Jobs? What shape will ministry towards
Job need to take now?

3. Job's wife (2:9–10)

*His wife said to him, 'Are you still holding on to your integrity?
Curse God and die!'*
*[10]He replied, 'You are talking like a foolish woman. Shall we
accept good from God, and not trouble?'*
In all this, Job did not sin in what he said.

Job's wife now comes on stage, or perhaps she has been there all
the time, but silent and puzzled. Now she comes into the limelight.

---

[10] Andersen, p. 86.
[11] C. S. Lewis, *A Grief Observed* (Faber, 1961), p. 23. (Originally published under
the pseudonym N. W. Clerk in 1961.) [12] Dt. 29:29.

27

Or, to change the metaphor, the camera angle widens to include not only Job but his social context also.

Job's desperate plight provokes his wife to cry out, 'Are you still holding on to your integrity? Curse God and die!' (2:9).

What are we to make of this? Is this one further fling of the Satan's style of temptation: Give up on God!

Or are we here simply seeing the wife's own misery? It is so hard to live near to someone who is suffering and to be utterly unable to do anything. Our own frustration is often turned to irritation with the one who is in pain: we blame the suffering person for causing us such discomfort. Job's wife suggests that he is as one already dead: why not cut the remaining suffering short by cursing God and provoking him to strike Job down?

Or is this genuine sympathy, longing for Job not to suffer any more? Or again, is Job's wife really angry with God for allowing or even causing such pain? This is, after all, the instinctive reaction of many of us.

Anger with God

Anger with God is a very common reaction to disaster. After the tragedy at Aberfan in Wales when a coal tip slid down on to a village school killing many children in their classrooms, one person after another was heard to say that they were 'so angry with God'. The same reaction is felt when a friend suffers the bereavement of a cot death. Christian friends, not knowing what to do with their feelings, are angry with God. Was this the sort of anger Job's wife felt?

The positive point to take from the reaction of Job's wife is that it, like Job's, is directed Godwards. The deep human emotion is at least expressed before God. The prophet Habakkuk does the same in his prayer of anger against God for allowing the rise of the Chaldean oppressors. He rails against God:

> How long, O LORD, must I call for help,
>   but you do not listen? . . .
> Why do you tolerate wrong?[13]

Job's wife at least sees things in terms of what God is doing, which is more than can be said for some of Job's other associates later in the book. Anger can be a much healthier starting-point, if it is anger expressed in acknowledgment of God, than the denial of anger which so often plagues Christian people. There is a health-

---

[13] Hab. 1:2–3.

ier reality in Job's wife, even if she got it wrong, than in the 'peace at any price' version of Christian faith which simply refuses to accept that good people can and do get angry.

That said, however, it did not help Job very much. In fact, what an additional burden it must have placed on him to find that at this crucial moment he and his wife were out of step. Job calls her foolish (2:10). For him, she is adding temptation to affliction. He knew (1:5) that it was a sin to curse God. Whatever later on in the story clouds Job's vision, at this point he sees clearly. At this point at least he did not sin.

4. Suffering presence (2:11–13)

When Job's three friends, Eliphaz the Temanite, Bildad the Shuhite and Zophar the Naamathite, heard about all the troubles that had come upon him, they set out from their homes and met together by agreement to go and sympathise with him and comfort him. ¹²*When they saw him from a distance, they could hardly recognise him; they began to weep aloud, and they tore their robes and sprinkled dust on their heads.* ¹³*Then they sat on the ground with him for seven days and seven nights. No-one said a word to him, because they saw how great his suffering was.*

Now follows one of the most moving paragraphs in the whole book of Job. If for the most part Job's friends got things wrong (as we shall see), here at the beginning they do it right. Together 'they set out from their homes and met together by agreement to go and sympathise with him and comfort him' (2:11). Their friendship was such as to bind them to Job even in his suffering and pain. But when they saw him they could hardly recognize him. Words which are used in the second part of Isaiah to describe the Servant of the Lord do not seem out of place as a description of the friends' reaction to Job:

> He had no beauty or majesty to attract us to him,
>   nothing in his appearance that we should desire him.
> He was despised and rejected by men,
>   a man of sorrows, and familiar with suffering.
> Like one from whom men hide their faces
>   he was despised . . . ¹⁴

So the friends offered traditional gestures of grief: they began to

¹⁴ Cf. Is. 53:2–3.

weep aloud, tore their robes and sprinkled dust on their heads. Then, amazingly, 'they sat on the ground with him for seven days and seven nights. No-one said a word to him, because they saw how great his suffering was' (2:13).

Silence

Here is genuine friendship. Here is deep ministry. This is what Stanley Hauerwas, in a book of this title, calls 'suffering presence'. Indeed, Hauerwas quotes this paragraph from Job as an introduction to one of his chapters in which he tells of his own ministry to a friend whose mother had just committed suicide:

> As often as I have reflected on what happened in that short space of time I have also remembered how inept I was in helping Bob. I did not know what could or should be said. I did not know how to help him start sorting out such a horrible event so that he could go on. All I could do was be present. But time has helped me to realise that this is all he wanted, namely my presence. For as inept as I was, my willingness to be present was a sign that this was not an event so horrible that it drew us away from all other human contact. Life could go on . . .
> I now think that at that time God granted me that marvellous privilege of being a presence in the face of profound pain and suffering, even when I did not appreciate the significance of being present.[15]

The compassion of a silent presence is what we here see in Job's friends. Theirs is a silence more eloquent than words, for there was nothing then to be said.

Craig Dykstra has put it well:

> Presence is a service of vulnerability. To be present to others is to put oneself in the position of being vulnerable to what they are vulnerable to, and of being vulnerable to them. It means being willing to suffer what the other suffers, and to go with the sufferer in his or her own suffering. This is different from trying to become the sufferer. Presence does not involve taking another's place. That would be demeaning. It would suggest, 'I can take your suffering better than you can, so move aside; I will replace you.' Instead, presence involves exposing oneself to

---

[15] S. Hauerwas, *Suffering Presence: Theological Reflections on Medicine, the Mentally Handicapped and the Church* (2nd ed., T. & T. Clark, 1988), pp. 64–65.

what the sufferer is exposed to, and being with the other in that vulnerability.[16]

Bishop John V. Taylor closes *The Go-Between God* (his vivid description of the Holy Spirit) with these paragraphs:

A colleague has recently described to me an occasion when a West Indian woman in a London flat was told of her husband's death in a street accident. The shock of grief stunned her like a blow, she sank into a corner of the sofa and sat there rigid and unhearing. For a long time her terrible tranced look continued to embarrass the family, friends and officials who came and went. Then the schoolteacher of one of her children, an Englishwoman, called, and seeing how things were, went and sat beside her. Without a word she threw an arm around the tight shoulders, clasping them with her full strength. The white cheek was thrust hard against the brown. Then as the unrelenting pain seeped through to her the newcomer's tears began to flow, falling on their two hands linked in the woman's lap. For a long time that is all that was happening. And then at last the West Indian woman started to sob. Still not a word was spoken and after a little while the visitor got up and went, leaving her contribution to help the family meet its immediate needs.

That is the embrace of God, his kiss of life. That is the embrace of his mission and of our intercession. And the Holy Spirit is the force in the straining muscles of an arm, the film of sweat between pressed cheeks, the mingled wetness on the backs of clasped hands. He is as close and unobtrusive as that, and as irresistibly strong.[17]

Suffering presence is the powerful ministry of silent compassion.

5. The purpose of the prologue

So far in the book of Job, the narrative has been prose. From chapter 3 to chapter 41 we move into poetry, and then at the end there is a prose epilogue again. Much of the heart of the book is the poem, dealing with Job's feelings, his friends' reactions, Job's responses, and the eventual speech from Yahweh himself. So why are we given this prose prologue? As we have said, it sets the scene within which the drama of the poem takes place. But it does more.

---

[16] C. Dykstra, *Vision and Character* (Paulist Press, 1981), p. 102.
[17] J. V. Taylor, *The Go-Between God* (SCM Press, 1972), p. 243.

Following Edgar Jones in *The Triumph of Job*, we can underline at least the following five features of the prologue, which contribute to our understanding of the rest of the book.

First, chapters 1 to 2 'put out of court the view that all suffering must be due to sin'.[18] We, the readers, know that Job was not being punished for his sins. Sometimes, of course, the Bible indicates that suffering is due to sin. Miriam is struck with leprosy for hers.[19] A failure to partake of the Holy Communion in an appropriately worthy and prepared manner is understood to be the cause of some people's weakness and illness in Corinth.[20] But again and again in the Bible, and nowhere more clearly than in the book of Job, we are warned against making too easy an equation between a person's suffering and their own sins. Jones rightly says that 'as a complete answer to explain every situation of suffering, the punitive concept of suffering is invalid'.[21]

Secondly, it is also clearly wrong to imagine, as Job's friends later do, that Job is being disciplined so that he may learn the error of his ways. Twice we are told of God's view of Job: that he was 'blameless and upright'. This prepares us for the assessment we will have to make of his friends' contributions in the next chapters. It also rules out the thought that Job's character is somehow being purified through his sufferings.

Thirdly, even though the book makes plain that good and upright people do suffer in this world without any apparent reason to account for it, the prologue, and indeed the rest of the book of Job, point us to the view that the outcome of such suffering will be a deeper relationship between the sufferer and God.

So, fourthly, the prologue invites us to place the problem of innocent suffering in a wider context. There are larger issues here than the question of suffering, serious though that is. How is a person to maintain faith in God in the face of suffering? That is the broader religious context of this book, the deeper issue at stake. We are being prepared here in the prologue not only to face the questions of suffering, but also to see them in the larger framework of Job's relationship with God.

Finally, Jones comments that 'in the transference of the scene from earth to heaven, we have a hint that even unconsciously men can be the vehicle of God's purposes'.[22] The suffering of human beings finds its meaning within God's heavenly purposes for his world. In the suffering of Job, God's servant, God is working out his purposes of grace. In that sense, Job will stand as a witness to

---

[18] Jones, p. 33.   [19] Nu. 12:10–12.   [20] 1 Cor. 11:30.   [21] Jones, p. 33.
[22] *Ibid.*, p. 34.

the truth which comes to its fullness in the life and death of Jesus Christ. For Christ, much more fully and marvellously than Job, is the Suffering Servant of the Lord. As H. Wheeler Robinson remarks, 'The Book of Job is . . . a first draft of the Gospel story, for it shows a man who bore his cross before Christ.'[23]

6. Job's lament (3:1–26)

After this, Job opened his mouth and cursed the day of his birth.
²He said:

> ³*'May the day of my birth perish,*
> *and the night it was said, "A boy is born!"*
> ⁴*That day – may it turn to darkness;*
> *may God above not care about it;*
> *may no light shine upon it.*
> ⁵*May darkness and deep shadow claim it once more;*
> *may a cloud settle over it;*
> *may blackness overwhelm its light.*
> ⁶*That night   may thick darkness seize it;*
> *may it not be included among the days of the year*
> *nor be entered in any of the months.*
> ⁷*May that night be barren;*
> *may no shout of joy be heard in it.*
> ⁸*May those who curse the days curse that day,*
> *those who are ready to rouse Leviathan.*
> ⁹*May its morning stars become dark;*
> *may it wait for daylight in vain*
> *and not see the first rays of dawn,*
> ¹⁰*for it did not shut the doors of the womb on me*
> *to hide trouble from my eyes.*
>
> ¹¹*'Why did I not perish at birth,*
> *and die as I came from the womb?*
> ¹²*Why were there knees to receive me*
> *and breasts that I might be nursed?*
> ¹³*For now I would be lying down in peace;*
> *I would be asleep and at rest*
> ¹⁴*with kings and counsellors of the earth,*
> *who built for themselves places now lying in*
> *ruins,*

---

[23] H. Wheeler Robinson, *The Cross in the Old Testament* (SCM Press, 1955), p. 54.

> ^{15}*with rulers who had gold,*
> *who filled their houses with silver.*
> ^{16}*Or why was I not hidden in the ground like a*
> *stillborn child,*
> *like an infant who never saw the light of day?*
> ^{17}*There the wicked cease from turmoil,*
> *and there the weary are at rest.*
> ^{18}*Captives also enjoy their ease;*
> *they no longer hear the slave driver's shout.*
> ^{19}*The small and the great are there,*
> *and the slave is freed from his master.*
>
> ^{20}*'Why is light given to those in misery,*
> *and life to the bitter of soul,*
> ^{21}*to those who long for death that does not come,*
> *who search for it more than for hidden treasure,*
> ^{22}*who are filled with gladness*
> *and rejoice when they reach the grave?*
> ^{23}*Why is life given to a man*
> *whose way is hidden,*
> *whom God has hedged in?*
> ^{24}*For sighing comes to me instead of food;*
> *my groans pour out like water.*
> ^{25}*What I feared has come upon me;*
> *what I dreaded has happened to me.*
> ^{26}*I have no peace, no quietness;*
> *I have no rest, but only turmoil.'*

Finally, the silence is broken. From the numbed shock of seven silent days and seven silent nights, as with a shriek, Job breaks the silence himself. He is not a dumb animal. He is a human being with thoughts and emotions. Perhaps the silence was now becoming misconstrued. Perhaps Job considered that it was endangering his integrity. Perhaps he felt he was being judged as in some way deserving his suffering. So he must protest – and protest he does.

After two chapters of the prose prologue, chapter 3 is the start of a long poem. Now we are taken inside Job's heart and made to feel his anguish. The cause of his pain is not so much his loss or his bereavement, his illness or his wife's tempting words. It is much more the absence and silence of God which troubles him now. Here is humanity's protest against the ways of God. Here Job is trying desperately to get his experience and his faith together. He is attempting to allow his faith to interpret his shocking experience. He cannot understand what has happened – what God has allowed to happen. What God is doing hurts desperately. But Job holds on in despairing faith that God is none the less a God of integrity, justice and truth.

Despair

So Job's feelings can only be couched in terms of despair about his own life. The lament is all expressed in the light of his faith in God, but his deep anguish remains unabated.

There are three main paragraphs to chapter 3.

i. Verses 3–10

Job here curses the day he was born. He does not curse God, or himself, or anyone else. He just wants the day of his birth blotted from the memory. May there be no remaining sense of joy and celebration at his birth – let the day rather be cursed.

Everything now is so wearisome. The full power of his lonely isolation hits him, and he bellows his misery.

ii. Verses 11–19

Then follows a series of questions. Why did he not perish at birth (3:11)? Why was there someone there to nurse him, rather than let him die in peace (3:12)? Why was his not a stillbirth (3:16)? Why do those who long to be delivered from life have to go on living (3:20)? Why does life have to continue for one who feels trapped by God (3:23)?

Why, why, why? O Lord, why?

Surely we know people who have asked that question. Surely we have asked it ourselves. And we know that for some such questions, as Lesslie Newbigin reminded us at the beginning of our chapter, there is no answer – at least not this side of heaven. From our side of the cross of Christ and the empty tomb of resurrection we may be enabled to bear those questions in a different light, for we know – as Job then did not – that there is One who stands beside us who has himself cried out, 'My God, my God, why . . . ?'[24] In his cry of dereliction on the cross, Jesus Christ has taken our questions on to his own lips, and made them his own. As Helmut Thielicke put it: 'At the bottom of every abyss he stands beside me.'[25]

But for Job, at this stage, there is just the question 'Why?' Could he not go to the place of Sheol, the place of the dead, the place of relief? (3:13–15).

[24] See Mt. 27:46; Mk. 15:34.
[25] H. Thielicke, *I Believe* (Collins, 1969), p. 117.

35

iii. Verses 20–26

Job ends his lament with a cry of reproach and bewilderment. Here he is getting close to the danger area where his faith in God's goodness is being pushed to its limit, and where, if he goes much further, he may deny that God is good. But, so far, he does not go over that limit; he does not abandon his faith. He cannot, though, understand why the result of God's gift of life should be that those who have it want to be rid of it. He feels 'hedged in' (3:23). This is not the sort of 'hedge' of which the Satan spoke in 1:10. There Job was depicted as hedged into a place of safety and security, protected from evil and suffering. His goodness was a false security, said Satan, because he had life too easy. But the hedge that Job now feels is the imprisonment of despair. Depression is beginning to take over. He is in God's trap, and there is no way out.

So sighing and groaning are his food and drink (3:24). He has a fear of being abandoned by God (3:25). The chapter ends with four sharp cries, as if in response to the four dagger stabs of pain earlier.

> 'I have no peace; no quietness;
> I have no rest, but only turmoil.'
>
> (3:26)

Or, as Andersen translates the verse:

> 'I cannot relax!
> And I cannot settle!
> And I cannot rest!
> And agitation keeps coming back!'[26]

Here is a severe anxiety state; the man is in great pain. He believes that God has grievously let him down. His sorrow goes on and on. It is terrible to watch. It is so unfair!

Coleridge once criticized many Christians for believing not in God himself, but for believing only in their beliefs about him. Great suffering puts an end to belief in beliefs. So far, Job is still holding on to his belief in God – but only just.

Indeed, as Karl Barth comments:

his true sorrow in all his sorrows, and therefore the primary subject of his complaints, consists in the conjunction of his profound knowledge that in what has happened and what has come

---

[26] Andersen, p. 110.

on him he has to do with God, and his no less profound ignorance how far he has to do with God.[27]

In other words, Job's knowledge of God and his ignorance of God's ways come into conflict.

The tension of faith

What we know of God and his goodness, and what we do not know about the mystery of God's heavenly purposes are here in headlong collision. There is an unbearable tension. 'This is the depth and essence of the suffering of the suffering Job.'[28] Job knows that his life is in the hands of God, and is lived in the faith that God is a good God. But in his actual experiences of life recently, he finds it impossible to see in what sense God has in fact got his well-being in mind. In all his overwhelming misfortunes he is sure that he is still in touch with God, but it is not the God he thought he knew. The God he is now experiencing seems more like an enemy than a friend, more like darkness than light. God is now *Deus absconditus*, the hidden God, whose presence is known only in the darkness of his absence. Can this still be the same God that he has served all these years? To quote Barth again, 'He does not doubt for a moment that he has to do with this God. But it almost drives him mad that he encounters him in a form in which he is absolutely alien.'[29] What has God become for him? – that is where the book of Job has brought us now.

The author has also brought us to the point where he seems to be saying to us, the readers: How would you help this man? What are you going to say? How can you minister to his deep needs? What does your theology say of someone like this? How are you going to keep believing in God in the face of such intolerable suffering? Are you believing only in beliefs, or will your trust in God himself stand the magnitude of this suffering? And how are you going to reconcile the presence of God with his apparent absence?

Unless the suffering of such as Job drives us back to the God who makes himself personally known, we will be missing the main things this book is written to teach.

How his friends responded to these questions, we will explore in our next chapter.

[27] K. Barth, *Church Dogmatics*, IV/3 (T. & T. Clark), p. 401.
[28] *Ibid.*, p. 401.   [29] *Ibid.*, p. 402.

WHY LORD?

Why Lord is there no-one?
No-one who cares.
The emptiness and bitterness
grow with passing years.

Why Lord can't I love?
Just anyone will do.
Someone who thinks I'm special.
Not only you.

Why Lord is there nothing?
Nothing to call mine.
Why Lord is there nowhere?
Nowhere to go.
Why Lord don't they want me?
Not even one.
Why Lord do they leave me?
Ever alone.

Will you go too, Lord?
Or were you ever there?
Created of necessity
to be someone to care.

Elizabeth Stewart

2. Speeches from Job's friends
(See Job 4 – 27)[1]

We left Job crying out to God in reproach for his circumstances: bereft, bewildered and in pain. He is still sitting on the ash heap outside the city scraping his sores, and his three friends have been with him for seven days and seven nights, the traditional period of time for mourning the dead.

In chapter 3, Job opened his mouth to break the long silence, and we heard the depths of his lament. Now his friends feel bound to reply.

The text of the book of Job between chapters 4 and 27 is divided into three cycles of speeches. Eliphaz speaks and Job replies; Bildad speaks and Job replies; Zophar speaks and Job replies. The cycle is repeated a second time, and then a third. Much of the text of the third cycle seems disordered and confused. In our Bibles, Bildad gets only a few verses in this third cycle and Zophar none at all. Some Old Testament specialists have rearranged the pattern, and allocated part of chapter 26 to Bildad, and part of chapter 27 to a third speech of Zophar. This certainly maintains the symmetry of the pattern of speeches, but has to remain speculative.

It may be, of course, that the friends were gradually spluttering into silence. It is certainly the case that Bildad and Zophar add very little in their second speeches to what they had urged in the first, and the incomplete third cycle could well reflect not only their running out of steam but also their running out of patience!

Outline of Job 4 – 27

At all events, chapters 4 to 27 of the book of Job as they have come to us can be outlined as follows:

[1] The speeches of Job's friends occur in Job 4 – 5; 8; 11; 15; 18; 20; 22; 25; ?26:5–14; ?27:13–23.

The three friends' speeches:			*Job's replies:*
Eliphaz	chs. 4 – 5		6 – 7
	15		16 – 17
	22		23 – 24
Bildad	8		9–10
	18		19
	25	(??26:5–14)	26 – 27
Zophar	11		12–14
	20		21
		(??27:13–23)	

(The sections in brackets indicate those passages on which commentators disagree, some allocating them to Bildad or Zophar, others holding to the allocation as it comes to us in our Bibles, namely that these are parts of the speeches of Job.)

In this second chapter, we concentrate on Eliphaz, Bildad and Zophar, scanning through their speeches as they occur in chapters 4 to 27.

In our third chapter, we will come back to these same chapters of the book of Job, concentrating that time on Job's responses. Then we will move on to chapters 29 to 31 (returning later to chapter 28, for reasons which will become clear in the fourth chapter).

Note The full biblical text of the speeches of Eliphaz, Bildad and Zophar is printed out in the Appendix at the end of this book (see pp. 165–178). The reader is encouraged to read this biblical text before proceeding with the discussion of the various friends' speeches.

1. The three friends: Eliphaz, Bildad and Zophar

The book of Job paints the frustrating picture of three well-meaning friends, trying to minister to a depressed person. It is frustrating because the first rule of ministry to people who are depressed is that you will almost certainly get it wrong.

You cook their favourite meal, you tidy the kitchen while they are out, you put fresh flowers in the hall, you even suggest that they have a new coat. All are wrong. You were supposed to realize that their present loss of appetite means that the sight of their favourite meal would reduce them to tears. Tidying the kitchen was actually a way of saying to them that you dislike the way they leave the kitchen in chaos. Putting fresh flowers in the hall was wrong, because they will die, and they looked so much prettier on the rockery. And as for suggesting a new coat – that was a threat because you are probably saying that they should at least try to do something about their dishevelled appearance, however low they feel.[2]

In one sense, Job's three friends, trying to minister to a depressed person, are therefore bound to get it wrong. But their getting it wrong is not only because of Job's state of mind. They get it wrong in a deeper sense also, as we shall see. We will need to ask serious questions about the theological ground on which they are standing as they make their responses to Job, and also about the practical and pastoral conclusions to which they come.

So first let us see if we can get the measure of Eliphaz.

2. Eliphaz

a. Eliphaz's first speech (Job 4 - 5)
(See pp. 165–168.)

Eliphaz's speeches start in Job 4. Eliphaz seems to be the oldest, profoundest, gentlest and generally nicest of the three friends. He has a deep faith in God's transcendent holiness, and a deep experience of God making himself known.

Here he is faced with his suffering friend. He has witnessed a profound and sudden change in Job's fortunes, from one who was so rich to one who has now become so poor. He has heard the terrible outburst of chapter 3 – but he knows nothing of the secret goings-on between God and the Satan in the heavenly court. Now he ventures to reply to Job's lament:

> [2]*If someone ventures a word with you, will you be*
> *impatient?*
> *But who can keep from speaking?*
> [3]*Think how you have instructed many,*
> *how you have strengthened feeble hands.*
> [4]*Your words have supported those who stumbled;*
> *you have strengthened faltering knees.*
> [5]*But now trouble comes to you, and you are discouraged;*

[2] From an unpublished paper by Sue Atkinson.

> *it strikes you, and you are dismayed.*
> *⁶Should not your piety be your confidence*
> *and your blameless ways your hope?*

(4:2–6)

Eliphaz ventures to speak

In this first speech, Eliphaz recognizes Job's true piety and good-ness. He recognizes that in days gone by Job has 'instructed many' (4:3), and has 'strengthened faltering knees' (4:4). Job has been known as someone who cares for those in trouble. He is a man of 'piety' and 'blameless ways' (4:6). Job has been in touch with the suffering of others. 'But now trouble comes to you' (4:5).

Eliphaz tries to encourage Job to be more confident, and to live in hope (4:6), for is it not the case that innocent and upright people are actually kept safe by God (4:7)? He bases his comfort on the belief that the righteous are not ultimately destroyed, the innocent do not perish (4:7):

> *⁷Consider now: Who, being innocent, has ever perished?*
> *Where were the upright ever destroyed?*
> *⁸As I have observed, those who plough evil*
> *and those who sow trouble reap it.*
> *⁹At the breath of God they are destroyed;*
> *at the blast of his anger they perish.*

(4:7–9)

'You reap what you sow'

We need to remind ourselves at this point of the theological view, shared by Eliphaz and the other friends, and by Job also, which is expressed in Job 4:8: 'Those who plough evil and those who sow trouble reap it.' You reap what you sow. That is the position on which Eliphaz is building his argument. Behind this theological principle is a view of the world as an ordered moral universe. God is a just God and a good God. Virtue will be rewarded, and the way of the wicked will perish.[3]

And of course, so far, so good. So far Eliphaz is perfectly right. This is a moral universe. As the psalmist in Psalm 1 made clear, there is a basic choice between godliness and the way of the wicked. There is no third option. And, as Jesus underlines more vividly in the Sermon on the Mount, there is a 'beatitude' on those who are in the right with God.[4]

---

[3] *Cf.* Ps. 1:6.　　[4] Mt. 5:3ff.

Many biblical writers pick up this theme. The First Letter of Peter draws on Psalm 34:12–16:

> the eyes of the Lord are on the righteous
> and his ears are attentive to their prayer,
> but the face of the Lord is against those who do evil.[5]

Jesus himself says, 'With the measure you use, it will be measured to you',[6] and Paul illustrates the same theme when he says, 'Do not be deceived: God cannot be mocked. A man reaps what he sows.'[7]

There is a principle of moral order in the world. There will be moral judgment. So let us never lose heart in striving to do what is good. That is the basic application of this faith. Although the gospel of grace in the New Testament reminds us that if we are united with Christ there is no longer any condemnation in the face of God's moral law,[8] this does not remove that other strand of Paul's theology: namely that Christians are judged according to their works.[9] It matters how we live. We reap what we sow.

In this sense, as we have said, Eliphaz is perfectly right. He reminds Job that he lives in a moral universe, and that godliness will bring its good reward.

Logic is not enough

However, in another sense, Eliphaz gets it entirely wrong. For he wrongly believes that this theological principle works the other way round: that everything you reap must result from something you have sown. This is manifestly untrue of Job. Eliphaz is here replacing theology with causal logic. He is taking a right theological principle and turning it on its head in a way which is both wrong, and unfair.

We need to be quite clear what is going on. The view that we reap what we sow is really a statement of faith. We believe that God is a good and sovereign Creator who knows what is best for his people. We believe that he judges the world justly. However, from our vantage point, we do not always know what is best for us, nor can we see how God is ruling his world. In fact what we see often seems to contradict our faith in the goodness of God. We cry out with the psalmist in Psalm 73:

[5] 1 Pet. 3:12.   [6] Mk. 4:24.   [7] Gal. 6:7.   [8] Rom. 8:1.
[9] 1 Cor. 3:10–15.

43

> I envied the arrogant
> when I saw the prosperity of the wicked.[10]

There is in other words, as we saw in the previous chapter, a dark
side to the reality of faith. But despite this dark side, we none the
less hold firm to the faith that God rewards good and punishes
evil. When Eliphaz affirms this (you reap what you sow), he is
right. But when he turns the credal statement of Psalm 1 upside
down, and so affirms, 'Because, Job, you are reaping disaster, you
must have sown iniquity', he has left faith in the living God in
favour of logic.

Eliphaz's narrow vision

Eliphaz seems unable to allow God to be the judge of rewards and
punishments, or even to allow that some principle other than
rewards and punishments may be in operation. He insists on inter-
preting what he sees before his eyes as evidence of God's mind.
But as Psalm 73 makes clear, God's actions and providences do not
necessarily fit in with our immediate expectancies. God is working
to purposes of his own. It is only when the psalmist could see
things from the perspective of eternity that he began to understand.[11] Eliphaz fails to distinguish between an earthly and a heavenly perspective. He operates with an easy natural view of causes
and effects – that a visible 'effect' (Job's suffering) must come from
an obvious cause (Job's sin). So Job ought to stop protesting his
innocence, and rather take responsibility for the sins which must,
Eliphaz insists, lie behind his present sufferings.

This faulty equation of particular sufferings with particular sins
results from the faulty process of arguing from one limited theological truth towards an unwarranted logical conclusion. Living faith
in the all-sovereign, good and gracious God has become rationalized into a dead orthodoxy based on a theory of natural causes.

We must beware of applying our causal logic to the ways of
God. As Pascal once said:

> Reason's last step is the recognition that there are an infinite
> number of things which are beyond it. It is merely feeble if it
> does not go as far as to realize that. If natural things are beyond
> it, what are we to say about supernatural things?[12]

We need to keep the doctrine of retributive justice within the
broader context of God's loving and often unexpected grace.

---

[10] Ps. 73:3.   [11] Ps. 73:17.   [12] B. Pascal, *Pensées* (Penguin ed., 1966), p. 85.

The evil results of turning living faith into cold logic are also seen in the Eliphazes of the present time who are found in the prosperity movements within the Christian churches. They tend to concentrate on righteousness and riches rather than on sin and suffering, but the process is the same. They argue that because God blesses the righteous, material prosperity is therefore a sign of divine blessing, and therefore something we should seek. We do not have to travel very far before we find the quest for material prosperity replacing the quest for godliness and righteousness of life. It is the Eliphaz mistake all over again, though in a different form. Faith in the living God has been replaced by a twisted logic. The moral universe of the gracious all-sovereign Creator God has been replaced by a smaller universe of natural causes, and material values.

Fellow travellers down this road include all those whose politics tempt them to equate material prosperity with the good life, and who see the poor and disadvantaged as themselves entirely to blame for their plight. It is all part of the Eliphaz logic which suggests that 'pull yourself together' is the only response to suffering and deprivation.

Eliphaz's vision

The sadness about Eliphaz is that he even claims to be given his views by divine revelation. Verses 12–21 of Job 4 describe an unusual mystical religious experience in which Eliphaz, through dreams and visions, is made aware of the ways of God.

> [12]*A word was secretly brought to me,*
>   *my ears caught a whisper of it.*
> [13]*Amid disquieting dreams in the night,*
>   *when deep sleep falls on men,*
> [14]*fear and trembling seized me*
>   *and made all my bones shake.*
> [15]*A spirit glided past my face,*
>   *and the hair on my body stood on end.*
> [16]*It stopped,*
>   *but I could not tell what it was.*
> *A form stood before my eyes,*
>   *and I heard a hushed voice:*
> [17]*"Can a mortal be more righteous than God?*
>   *Can a man be more pure than his Maker?"*
>
>   (4:12–17)

These verses carry a rather eerie build-up to what we expect to be

45

a climactic revelation. When it comes it is rather flat! 'Can a mortal be more righteous than God?' (4:17). No, Job, you must learn to take responsibility for your sins.

So here we see Eliphaz responding to Job by speaking just part of the truth. He tells Job that it is useless to go on with his appeal: 'Call if you will, but who will answer you? To which of the holy ones will you turn?' (5:1). Job must recognize his mortality and his share in the universal sinfulness of humanity. At this point Eliphaz is underlining standard wisdom teaching (5:6–7) that 'man is born to trouble as surely as sparks fly upward'. This is the general law of experience: is it even a sort of cosmic fatalism?

Job must stop indulging his grief and protesting his innocence. He must rather lift up his eyes to the transcendent God. 'If it were I,' says Eliphaz, 'I would appeal to God; I would lay my cause before him' (5:8). Not, that is, in terms of protest, but by Job reminding himself of God's creative power and justice. Job 5:9–16, which follows, is a hymn of praise to the goodness of God.

Eliphaz extols the goodness of God
> ⁹*He performs wonders that cannot be fathomed,*
>   *miracles that cannot be counted.*
> ¹⁰*He bestows rain on the earth;*
>   *he sends water upon the countryside.*
> ¹¹*The lowly he sets on high,*
>   *and those who mourn are lifted to safety.*
> ¹²*He thwarts the plans of the crafty,*
>   *so that their hands achieve no success.*
> ¹³*He catches the wise in their craftiness,*
>   *and the schemes of the wily are swept away.*
> ¹⁴*Darkness comes upon them in the daytime;*
>   *at noon they grope as in the night.*
> ¹⁵*He saves the needy from the sword in their mouth;*
>   *he saves them from the clutches of the powerful.*
> ¹⁶*So the poor have hope,*
>   *and injustice shuts its mouth.*

(5:9–16)

The whole of Eliphaz's argument is based on his view of the moral perfection of God, in the light of which Job must see he is in the wrong. Eliphaz is here so near, and yet – as we have seen, and shall see – so far.

Eliphaz on happiness
Eliphaz then moves to a discussion of the happiness of the person

who takes life's troubles in the right spirit. He sees suffering as a means by which God disciplines and chastens, and of course sometimes this is true. The writer to the Hebrews repeats the proverb that the Lord disciplines those he loves.[13] Eliphaz says much the same in 5:17–26. 'He wounds, but he also binds up; he injures, but his hands also heal' (5:18). But once again Eliphaz is wrong in applying this to Job. If only Job will admit his sin, he says, there can be happiness again. Job will know security again, his family will prosper again, and he will yet have a vigorous life before he dies (5:24–27). We may, in passing, notice the gross insensitivity of Eliphaz at this point. It is hardly appropriate to be telling someone who has lost his house and all his descendants in terrible circumstances, that his tent will be secure, and that he will have many children. Nor is it particularly helpful to be saying to someone who wants to die that his remaining years will be full of life. But apart from this, Eliphaz has been speaking part of the truth – though inappropriately.

The dark side of God

There is, however, a part of the truth that Eliphaz does not say: the part that is actually true of Job. It is the case that God, morally perfect and good as Eliphaz rightly says, does seem at times to turn his face away not only from the ungodly, but from good and righteous people also. Sometimes even good people experience the dark side of God.

Dr Martyn Lloyd-Jones puts it like this:

I remember the case of a lady who had been passing through one of these periods of dryness and aridity and who was in great trouble. It was partly physical, and many of her friends had gone to her, some of them being ministers of the Word, and they had all spoken in the same way. They were all trying to make her rouse herself, all talking in a theoretical manner to her and saying that feelings do not matter, that indeed nothing matters except the truth of justification by faith. She knew that quite as well as they did, better indeed than many of them, but that did not help her, for her problem was that she did not know the blessedness she once had known. 'Where is the blessedness I knew when first I saw the Lord?' That was her condition, the condition described by the poet William Cowper.

The advice of her friends did not help her, because it never helps such people to tell them to pull themselves together and

---

[13] See Heb. 12:5–11.

to rouse themselves. That is just what they cannot do ... The way to help such a person, the way in which the particular person to whom I am referring was helped, is to say 'Ah yes, you know, there are periods like that in the lives of the saints. Sometimes God for his own inscrutable reasons withholds his face from us.' She looked at me in amazement saying 'Is that true?' 'Of course it is true' I replied; and I proceeded to give her many examples and illustrations of it. At once her problem was solved, because she now had an explanation ... [14]

Sometimes God allows us to go through experiences in which his face seems turned away from us. Sometimes we learn in that way lessons of faith that we could never have learned in any other way. For Eliphaz to tell us at such times to pull ourselves together and take responsibility for our faults simply misses the point.

b. Eliphaz's second speech (Job 15)
(See pp. 168–170.)

Eliphaz rebukes Job

Eliphaz's second speech comes in chapter 15 after Bildad and Zophar have spoken, and Job has replied to each. Now Eliphaz begins to shift his ground. He begins by telling Job that it is ungodly to attack God (15:2–6). He pigeon-holes Job as 'godless', and directly accuses him of undermining the true life of piety and devotion to God (15:4). Moffat translates verse 4: 'You undermine religion, with your threatening of God.'

Then in 15:7–11, resentment seems to creep in to Eliphaz's response:

> [7]*Are you the first man ever born?*
> *Were you brought forth before the hills?*
> [8]*Do you listen in on God's council?*
> *Do you limit wisdom to yourself?*
> [9]*What do you know that we do not know?*
> *What insights do you have that we do not have?*
> [10]*The grey-haired and the aged are on our side,*
> *men even older than your father.*
> [11]*Are God's consolations not enough for you,*
> *words spoken gently to you?*

> (15:7–11)

[14] M. Lloyd-Jones, *Romans: An exposition of chapter 8:17–39: The Final Perseverance of the Saints* (Banner of Truth, 1975), p. 176.

Who does Job think he is?

Eliphaz seems to be saying to Job: Who on earth do you think you are? 'What do you know that we do not know? And what insights do you have that we do not have?' (15:9). God does not even regard his 'holy ones' as utterly trustworthy, so how dare you, Job, consider yourself righteous before God (15:15–16)?

Eliphaz then takes refuge once more in rationalization: 'Listen to me and I will explain to you; let me tell you what I have seen, what wise men have declared, hiding nothing received from their fathers' (15:17–18).

The traditional picture of the evil-doer

The wisdom of the wise is on his side: suffering goes with wickedness (15:20). This leads Eliphaz to a statement of the traditional picture of the evil-doer, which is spelled out in verses 20–35:

> ²⁰*All his days the wicked man suffers torment,*
> *the ruthless through all the years stored up for him.*
> ²¹*Terrifying sounds fill his ears;*
> *when all seems well, marauders attack him.*
> ²²*He despairs of escaping the darkness;*
> *he is marked for the sword.*
>
> ³⁴*For the company of the godless will be barren,*
> *and fire will consume the tents of those who love bribes.*
> ³⁵*They conceive trouble and give birth to evil;*
> *their womb fashions deceit.*
>
> (15:20–22, 34–35)

Here Eliphaz is drawing a picture of the wicked. The implication is that Job is among them. Job really 'vaunts himself against the Almighty' (15:25). No wonder things are going wrong.

c. Eliphaz's third speech (Job 22)
(See pp 170–171.)

Is God really concerned with Job?

The third speech from Eliphaz, in chapter 22, is another attempt in the light of Job's continuing protests to face Job with the almightiness of God. Eliphaz pushes this to the extreme of saying that God is so loftily transcendent that he is lifted right out of any direct concern with Job at all: Do you think God cares one way or the other about your protestation and your righteousness? God is not involved in the trivia of your life, what difference does it make to him either way? 'What pleasure would it give the Almighty if you were righteous? What would he gain if your ways were blameless?' (22:3). He then implies that because God is so disinterested, Job's anguish must be proof of his sin (22:5).

There is a nastiness about Eliphaz's tone which now seeps into the rest of his speech. He starts to manufacture 'evidence' against Job, accusing him of various sins. Job's wickedness, says Eliphaz, is great (22:5); Job has been unjust to his family (22:6), uncaring to the hungry and thirsty (22:7), lording it over the widows and the orphans (22:9). That is why Job is in torment now (22:10–11).

The good and godly Eliphaz has now gone right over the top. We may forgive his faulty theology – he was in line with the view widespread in his day and ours, expressed by all those who ask, 'What have I done that God has done this to me?' While theologically askew, it may reflect a basic human intuition that we live in a moral universe. But it is hard to forgive Eliphaz his unjust tirade. The conversation with Job in his suffering has taken its toll on Eliphaz, and his own frustrations at getting nowhere, and finding no answer, has clouded his judgment of the truth.

Eliphaz appeals to Job

Eliphaz finally appeals to Job to come back to God (22:21–30). He was right to make clear that repentance brings blessing: 'Submit to God and be at peace with him' (22:21). But, however moving we find Eliphaz's appeal, it is based on an utterly false view of Job's position. Eliphaz rightly realizes that Job's sufferings cannot be ended without the restoration of communion between Job and God (22:21), for that breakdown in fellowship is Job's deepest suffering of all. But he puts the whole task back on to Job's shoulders. This is the heresy of Pelagianism – putting the responsibility for our relationship with God solely in our own hands. Although Eliphaz extols the sovereignty of God in words, he says nothing about grace. His whole gospel reduces to telling Job to pull his socks up.

The nature of Eliphaz's approach

So what are we to make of Eliphaz?

He was good and God-fearing. For the most part he speaks the truth, or at least some of the truth. He speaks from experience of God's transcendence, magnifying God's moral perfection. He knows the power of repentance to bring blessing to a person. But through his narrow vision, he tries to handle Job's problem in terms of his own rationalizations. This leads him to argue that Job must really be making a fuss about nothing. Suffering is simply part of the way things are in the world. It is one of the ways God chastens and disciplines us. All evil-doers will suffer, in the long term if not in the short term. So do not trouble the Almighty with your trivia – simply repent, make your peace with him, and all will be well.

Eliphaz thus tries to help Job by side-stepping the depths of the problem. Job could properly feel that he had not really been *heard* by Eliphaz. Eliphaz comes over as rather pompous (5:8), insensitive (5:24), defensive (15:9–10), and he is rather too quick to accuse (22:5ff.). He does not and cannot catch the magnitude of Job's protest. Yes, says Job, I know that God chastens us by suffering, but I have nothing to be chastened for! Yes, I know God punishes evil, but I have done no evil on this scale at all! And, moreover, I believe that the Almighty God you proclaim *is* concerned about the details of life – what you call trivia. And *that is my problem*: why does he not *seem* to be concerned with *me*?

This is a theme picked up by Helmut Thielicke in his book on the Creed. He writes:

> Tell me how lofty God is for you, and I'll tell you how little he means to you. That could be a theological axiom. The lofty God has been lofted right out of my private life. It is certainly remarkable but it is true: God has become of concern to me *only* because he has made himself *smaller* than the Milky Way; only because he is present in my little sickroom when I gasp for breath, or understands the little cares I cast on him, or takes seriously the request of a child for a scooter with balloon tyres. He concerns me because Jesus Christ takes my speck of anxiety and my personal guilt upon himself.[15]

God is concerned with our 'trivia'. Job was nearer to the truth of Christ than Eliphaz.

3. Bildad

Bildad is different. He is the 'traditionalist par excellence'.[16] He goes by the book. His source of information is not experience (like Eliphaz), but his scholarship. Jones quotes Terrien's comment that Bildad's 'source of enlightenment is not a personal contact with a present God, but scholarly learning and archaeological hoarding',[17] and notes that Bildad is the type of theologian who appeals to the

---

[15] Thielicke, *I Believe*, p. 33.   [16] Jones, p. 49.   [17] Terrien, p. 973.

SPEECHES FROM JOB'S FRIENDS

past without realizing that the present requires the rethinking of formulas of previous generations which are no longer adequate.[18]

Here is a theologian who is quite well read, but who is entirely wedded to the past.

a. Bildad's first speech (Job 8)
(See pp. 172–173.)

Bildad's first speech comes in chapter 8, and opens with a note of annoyance against Job: 'How long will you say such things? Your words are a blustering wind' (8:2). He goes on to suggest that Job's children's deaths were their own fault (8:4). But he has a strong sense of God's power and God's justice:

> *³Does God pervert justice?*
> *Does the Almighty pervert what is right?*
> *⁴When your children sinned against him,*
> *he gave them over to the penalty of their sin.*
> *⁵But if you will look to God*
> *and plead with the Almighty,*
> *⁶if you are pure and upright,*
> *even now he will rouse himself on your behalf*
> *and restore you to your rightful place.*
> *⁷Your beginnings will seem humble,*
> *so prosperous will your future be.*
>
> (8:3–7)

The justice of God

Whereas Eliphaz extolled God's transcendent holiness, Bildad talks more about his power, and his unwavering justice. 'Does God pervert justice? Does the Almighty pervert what is right?' he asks (8:3). There is an inflexible righteous and just power in God. So Bildad's remedy for Job is to 'look to God'. If you will look to God, God will 'even now . . . rouse himself on your behalf and restore you to your rightful place' (8:6). Bildad knows there is something wrong in Job's relationship with God. He calls on Job to 'trust in the Lord', and in this he is surely right: much of the wisdom literature says the same.[19]

Appeal to ancient wisdom

In much of his speech, Bildad is simply reflecting the teaching of

[18] See Jones, p. 49.   [19] *Cf.* Pr. 3:5–6.

a long line of godly ancestors. He appeals to them in 8:8–10. Bildad
tells Job that things will improve. He includes the sombre note that
God's retribution against the wicked will be seen, although it may
take more than one generation to work through.

But God is just: God cannot do wrong. Look at the world
around you, says Bildad. Wickedness brings its own reward and it
is just as fragile as a spider's web (8:14), or like a plant (8:16),
thriving and firmly rooted for a while, but destroyed by the very
soil in which it grew.

> [11]*Can papyrus grow tall where there is no marsh?*
>   *Can reeds thrive without water?*
> [12]*While still growing and uncut,*
>   *they wither more quickly than grass.*
> [13]*Such is the destiny of all who forget God;*
>   *so perishes the hope of the godless.*
> [14]*What he trusts in is fragile;*
>   *what he relies on is a spider's web.*
> [15]*He leans on his web, but it gives way;*
>   *he clings to it, but it does not hold.*
> [16]*He is like a well-watered plant in the sunshine,*
>   *spreading its shoots over the garden;*
> [17]*it entwines its roots around a pile of rocks*
>   *and looks for a place among the stones.*
> [18]*But when it is torn from its spot,*
>   *that place disowns it and says, 'I never saw you.'*
> [19]*Surely its life withers away,*
>   *and from the soil other plants grow.*
>
>   (8:11–19)

So buck up, Job! It is going to be all right! 'Surely God does not
reject a blameless man . . . He will yet fill your mouth with laughter
and your lips with shouts of joy!' (8:20–22). Bildad quotes from
the lines we know as Psalms 126:2 and 132:18, to make his point
that everything will turn out for the best.

b. Bildad's second speech (Job 18)
(See pp. 173–174.)

The second speech from Bildad comes in chapter 18. After Job's
further replies, Bildad says in effect (18:2): 'Are you going to go
on talking for ever?' He urges Job to 'Be sensible' (18:2), as though
that was just the thing which Job needed to hear! Bildad gives way
to scorn (18:3): 'Why are we regarded as cattle and considered

stupid in your sight?' This leads him to another long tale of the fate of the wicked. Verses 5–21 tell of the insecurity, terror and hopelessness of the ungodly:

> ⁵*The lamp of the wicked is snuffed out;*
> *the flame of his fire stops burning.*
> ⁶*The light in his tent becomes dark;*
> *the lamp beside him goes out.*
> ⁷*The vigour of his step is weakened;*
> *his own schemes throw him down.*
> ⁸*His feet thrust him into a net*
> *and he wanders into its mesh.*
> ⁹*A trap seizes him by the heel;*
> *a snare holds him fast.*
> ¹⁰*A noose is hidden for him on the ground;*
> *a trap lies in his path.*
> ¹¹*Terrors startle him on every side*
> *and dog his every step.*
> ¹²*Calamity is hungry for him;*
> *disaster is ready for him when he falls.*
> ¹³*It eats away parts of his skin;*
> *death's firstborn devours his limbs.*
> ¹⁴*He is torn from the security of his tent*
> *and marched off to the king of terrors.*
> ¹⁵*Fire resides in his tent;*
> *burning sulphur is scattered over his dwelling.*
> ¹⁶*His roots dry up below*
> *and his branches wither above.*
> ¹⁷*The memory of him perishes from the earth;*
> *he has no name in the land.*
> ¹⁸*He is driven from light into darkness*
> *and is banished from the world.*
> ¹⁹*He has no offspring or descendants among his people,*
> *no survivor where once he lived.*
> ²⁰*Men of the west are appalled at his fate;*
> *men of the east are seized with horror.*
> ²¹*Surely such is the dwelling of an evil man;*
> *such is the place of one who knows not God.*
>
> (18:5–21)

The wicked man is driven from light into darkness; people are appalled at his fate. The implication here is that Job, in Bildad's eyes, is well on the way to becoming one of them. If only he would 'be sensible' and listen to the wisdom of others to guide him to a more acceptable frame of mind.

As with Eliphaz, Bildad's first speech concentrates on the nature of God, and his second applies this to the fate of the wicked, among whom he includes Job. Like Eliphaz, much of what Bildad says is true in general terms. But, as with Eliphaz, Bildad fails utterly to engage with Job's situation.

c. Bildad's third speech (Job 25)
(See pp. 174–175.)

According to several commentators, Bildad's third speech includes not only chapter 25, but also some unattributed verses in 26:5–14. But while the tone of the second part of chapter 26 seems to fit with Bildad in its celebration of God's creative power, it is perfectly possible that Job is asserting Bildad's views for himself, and then showing that they are not the answer to his personal riddle.

How can a person be righteous before this God?

What is unambiguously clear, however, is that chapter 25 begins with Bildad's marvellous statement about the divine power of God: 'Dominion and awe belong to God; he establishes order in the heights of heaven. Can his forces be numbered? Upon whom does his light not rise?' (25:2–3). Bildad then goes on to draw the conclusion that there can be no such thing as perfection on earth. 'How then can a man be righteous before God? How can one born of woman be pure?' (25:4).

The theme of God's awesome majesty is continued in 26:5–14 in a marvellous celebration of God's creative power, whether this is to be attributed to Bildad, or is part of Job's reply:

> 7He spreads out the northern skies over empty space;
>   he suspends the earth over nothing.
> 8He wraps up the waters in his clouds,
>   yet the clouds do not burst under their weight.
> 9He covers the face of the full moon,
>   spreading his clouds over it.
> 10He marks out the horizon on the face of the waters
>   for a boundary between light and darkness.
> 11The pillars of the heavens quake,
>   aghast at his rebuke.
> 12By his power he churned up the sea;
>   by his wisdom he cut Rahab to pieces.

55

> [13]*By his breath the skies became fair;*
> *his hand pierced the gliding serpent.*
>
> (26:7–13)

And these, the writer continues, 'are but the outer fringe of his works' (26:14). He even gives us a hint of a reverent agnosticism: 'How faint the whisper we hear of him! Who then can understand the thunder of his power?' (26:14–15).

Bildad misses the point

Bildad builds on faithful orthodoxy: God the Creator, God the just, God the omnipotent one. This is the God of Bildad's teachers, and of Bildad himself – a God of might, majesty, dominion and strength. Yet, like Eliphaz before him, Bildad has failed to meet Job where he really is. For Job held these beliefs in God as well, but whether or not Job believed was not the point at issue in this time of suffering and bewilderment. It was rather that his beliefs did not engage with his experience. For Job the questions are somewhere else. '*Why*', says Job, 'does your all-powerful God not come to *me*? Why does the God who reveals himself in nature not make himself known to *me*? Why does your just God not deal justly with *me*? Am I merely a puppet in the hands of omnipotence? Why do *I* not seem to matter any more?'

Listening

Bildad's inappropriate declaration of truth reminds us of the crucial importance of listening. This applies not only to counsellors, but also to those given the ministry of preaching. Bildad had not heard where Job was in his need. His counselling and his preaching, even when it was true, missed the point. We all know the sort of preaching which really engages with us, which meets us where we are, which indicates that the preacher has really understood the human condition, and is seeking to feel his way both into his text and into the hearts of his hearers, so that the preaching event is an engagement between the Word of God and the hearts of people. The Word then strikes home with prophetic power. It is an occasion on which we are changed, are brought into touch with the living God, and hear his Word spoken freshly where we are. We also know the sort of preaching which, though traditionally orthodox to a fault, is dry, detached, and floats in an academic cloud somewhere above our heads, not meeting us anywhere at all. The first is the authentic gift of preaching found in those who first exercise a ministry of listening. The second is the way of Bildad.

4. Zophar

Zophar is our third speaker, and he is rather a nasty piece of work. Zophar is high on the list of those without whom we could happily live if we never saw them again: an insolent, intellectual prig. He was one of those tiresome people – probably just out of College! – who know *everything*. As Robert Gordis says of him, 'He never lets facts interfere with his theories.'[20]

a. Zophar's first speech (Job 11)
(See pp. 175–176.)

Zophar rebukes Job

By this point in the book of Job, we have heard Eliphaz's first speech, to which Job gave a reply, and Bildad's first speech, to which Job also replied. Zophar is really very indignant at Job's continuing protest, and he accuses Job of idle prattle: 'Are all these words to go unanswered? Is this talker to be vindicated? Will your idle talk reduce men to silence? Will no-one rebuke you when you mock?' (11:2–3). His scornful rebuke to Job for continuing to protest his innocence and sense of injustice is recorded in verses 4–5: 'You say to God, "My beliefs are flawless and I am pure in your sight." Oh, how I wish that God would speak, that he would open his lips against you.'

Zophar extols God's wisdom

Then, in a speech of marvellous words, but overly patronizing in tone, Zophar continues:

> [7]*Can you fathom the mysteries of God?*
> *Can you probe the limits of the Almighty?*
> [8]*They are higher than the heavens – what can you do?*
> *They are deeper than the depths of the grave – what*
> *can you know?*
> [9]*Their measure is longer than the earth and wider than the*
> *sea.*
>
> (11:7–9)

Zophar should apply this to himself!

Zophar rests on God's omniscience and God's inscrutable wisdom, and of course on his own inalienable common sense. Zophar says that there are many things in the world which are a

[20] Gordis, p. 77.

mystery to us. But God remains just. Behind Zophar's view, as with Eliphaz's, is a view of the universe in which evil is punished. 'When he sees evil, does he not take note?' (11:11). But Zophar seems to turn this into a law of divine retaliation: You owe, so you must pay. He appeals to Job to repent.

The way of repentance

In verses 13–14 Zophar sets out four steps to repentance, and then the blessings that will follow:

> ¹³*Yet if you devote your heart to him*
> *and stretch out your hands to him,*
> ¹⁴*if you put away the sin that is in your hand*
> *and allow no evil to dwell in your tent,*
> ¹⁵*then you will lift up your face without shame;*
> *you will stand firm and without fear.*
> ¹⁶*You will surely forget your trouble,*
> *recalling it only as waters gone by.*
> ¹⁷*Life will be brighter than noonday,*
> *and darkness will become like morning.*
> ¹⁸*You will be secure, because there is hope;*
> *you will look about you and take your rest in safety.*
> ¹⁹*You will lie down, with no-one to make you afraid,*
> *and many will court your favour.*
>
> (11:13–19)

Step one is to 'devote your heart to him'; then, secondly, 'stretch out your hands to him' in supplication; thirdly, 'put away the sin that is in your hand', the sinful things which you are doing at the moment; and fourthly, 'allow no evil to dwell in your tent' – your whole context must be cleansed from sin. If you do these things, the blessings of the penitent will come to you.

Verses 15 – 19 paint a picture of these blessings: You will lift up your face without shame, you will stand firm and without fear, you will forget your trouble, and your life will be brighter than noonday; you will be secure because there is hope, you will rest in safety; you will lie down with no-one to make you afraid.

Zophar is right: the life of faith is to be based on penitence and obedience. Zophar is right: God does give the blessings of hope, security and peace to his people. But Zophar, like his friends, is only telling half the truth. He is wrong in forgetting that God also sometimes allows unpredictable and seemingly unfair suffering. He is wrong in presuming that the answer for Job is repentance.

But that is his message: if only Job would repent, his happiness would be restored. But if he won't, then he will go the way of the wicked (11:20). How cruelly Zophar misses Job's deepest needs, by failing – like the other friends – to see the reality of Job's situation.

b. Zophar's second speech (Job 20)
(See pp. 176–178.)

Zophar's impatience

Zophar's second speech, in chapter 20, is not much more help. With increasing impatience (20:2), Zophar tells Job again about the fate of the wicked. The gist of their fate comes at the end of the chapter:

> Terrors will come over him;
> ²⁶ total darkness lies in wait for his treasures.
> A fire unfanned will consume him
>   and devour what is left in his tent.
> ²⁷The heavens will expose his guilt;
>   the earth will rise up against him.
> ²⁸A flood will carry off his house,
>   rushing waters on the day of God's wrath.
> ²⁹Such is the fate God allots the wicked,
>   the heritage appointed for them by God.
>
> (20:25b–29)

If we follow the view of those commentators who think that *a third speech of Zophar's* is to be found in 27:13–23, the same theme occurs there:

> ¹³'Here is the fate God allots to the wicked,
>   the heritage a ruthless man receives from the Almighty:
> ¹⁴However many his children, their fate is the sword;
>   his offspring will never have enough to eat.
> ¹⁵The plague will bury those who survive him,
>   and their widows will not weep for them.
> ¹⁶Though he heaps up silver like dust
>   and clothes like piles of clay,
> ¹⁷what he lays up the righteous will wear,
>   and the innocent will divide his silver.
> ¹⁸The house he builds is like a moth's cocoon,
>   like a hut made by a watchman.
> ¹⁹He lies down wealthy, but will do so no more;

when he opens his eyes, all is gone.
[20]*Terrors overtake him like a flood;*
   a tempest snatches him away in the night.
[21]*The east wind carries him off, and he is gone;*
   it sweeps him out of his place.
[22]*It hurls itself against him without mercy*
   as he flees headlong from its power.
[23]*It claps its hands in derision*
   and hisses him out of his place.

(27:13–23)

Zophar seems altogether unsympathetic and unfeeling. He is a man full of his own importance and his own ideas, and utterly unable to engage with Job at his point of need.

Counselling

Zophar vividly illustrates the opposite of the effective counsellor! According to Charles Truax and Robert Carkhuff, who made a careful survey of the available literature,[21] there is an essential set of qualities for effective counselling. They single out genuineness, non-possessive warmth; and accurate empathy.

By 'genuineness' they mean a measure of self-awareness in the counsellor, who is aware of his own weaknesses, yet sufficiently secure in himself to help someone in difficulty. A 'genuine' counsellor is not unduly concerned with his own status or role. His respect for the counsellee must not be phoney.

By 'non-possessive warmth', Truax and Carkhuff mean the ability in the counsellor to communicate positive acceptance and genuine care. It means being non-judgmental (where 'judgmental' means condemning), but that does not mean being undiscriminating.[22]

By 'empathy' these authors mean the power in the counsellor of so standing where the counsellee stands that he or she understands the counsellee's situation and feelings without becoming submerged by them. It communicates: 'I am standing with you in your pain: I understand what you feel.' As Roger Hurding comments:

Sometimes the counsellor is readily empathetic because he too has suffered and has learnt through his suffering. Such an attribute can be seen in Paul's second letter to the Corinthians where he wrote:

[21] C. B. Truax and R. R. Carkhuff, *Towards Effective Counseling and Psychotherapy* (Aldine Publishing, 1967).
[22] *Cf.* R. F. Hurding, *Roots and Shoots* (Hodder & Stoughton, 1986), pp. 31ff.

'Blessed be the God and Father of our Lord Jesus Christ, the Father of mercies and God of all comfort, who comforts us in all our affliction, so that we may be able to comfort those who are in any affliction, with the comfort with which we ourselves are comforted by God.'[23]

Zophar, sadly, has little genuineness, even less warmth, and no empathy at all!

5. Summary of the three friends' views

We have explored the sweet-reasonableness of Eliphaz, the logician, who effectively places his rationalizations above faith in the living God. We have looked at Bildad, the traditionalist, the preacher, with his sharp tongue and narrow mind, who is more ready to speak than to listen. We have come face to face with Zophar, the arrogant counsellor, whose approach is marked by impetuosity and directive confrontation.

So where does all this take us? The three friends are telling the truth, at least in part. They are defending the view that this universe is governed by a God who is not only almighty but also just and good. This world rests on the holiness, justice and wisdom of God, they argue – and of course they are right. God's holiness, justice and wisdom are not simply the products of our own minds and feelings; they are objectively real. Perhaps the friends think Job is taking too much notice of his feelings. Faith not feelings! That's their message – there is an objective moral order in the universe: something outside ourselves by which we are judged.

So Eliphaz argues from his experience about God's transcendent holiness; Bildad argues from traditional orthodoxy about God's power and righteous justice; Zophar argues from an overdose of what he calls common sense about God's inscrutable and omniscient wisdom: they are all telling the truth – or at least part of it.

And yet they are missing Job in his need.

Different starting-points

We should pause here and notice one important difference between the three friends. All have begun with their conception of God, and all have moved on to the practical implications of their view of God for this pastoral need. And they are different. That seems to be of very significant pastoral importance. The picture we have

[23] *Ibid.*, p. 34, and quoting 2 Cor. 1:3–4, RSV.

of God, and the metaphors that guide our understanding of him are crucially important in the way we frame the moral and pastoral questions which confront us. If with Eliphaz we think of God primarily as holy, we will approach the pastoral situation in one way. If with Bildad we begin with God's justice, we will approach it another way. If, with Zophar, God's omniscience is the major theme, our approach will be different yet again.

In Richard Niebuhr's book *The Responsible Self*, he considers three primary approaches to the question of personal responsibility, in the light of the guiding metaphors for God.[24] Some begin with God as Creator, others with God as Reconciler, others with God as Redeemer. The moral questions then become, in each case, 'What is right?', 'What is good?', 'What is fitting?' The moral task is understood either as searching for principles of right action to guide our actions, or for guidelines in goodness to show us the way to the best consequences, or for an answer to the question of how we should act in response to God's action in the world. The various approaches to Christian ethics can be understood in terms of different guiding metaphors for God. Clearly all are important, and all have to be taken into account.

Our guiding metaphors for God dictate the ways our moral and pastoral questions are framed. If we begin with God as Creator and law-giver we may find ourselves talking mostly about obedience to divine commands, about sin and the need for repentance. If our starting-point is the compassion of God the Redeemer, we may see moral issues in terms of falling short of divine ideals and the journey of faith. If our starting-point is the love of God, we may primarily stress a personalistic ethic and the need for mutual acceptance and understanding. Many participants in various debates about personal morality, for example, never really engage with one another because their starting-points are different, and they are facing in different directions. The moral and pastoral conclusions we come to will depend to a very large degree on the guiding metaphors for God with which we start.

A warning

Job's three friends all think of God differently. They have all tried to help him, but all have failed. They stand as a clear warning to us that it is one thing to proclaim the truth about God; it is quite another thing to press the claims of truth inappropriately. For Eliphaz side-steps Job's problem by talking about something else. Bildad's view of the moral order is too narrow to include Job's

[24] H. R. Niebuhr, *The Responsible Self* (Harper & Row, 1979).

personal needs; Zophar believes he sees things more clearly than they really are. Maybe they could not bear to see their friend in, pain. Maybe they could not stick with his pain themselves.

They are all counsellors and preachers. Yet the Lord says to them at the end of the book: 'My wrath is kindled against you . . . for you have not spoken of me what is right' (42:7, RSV).

In effect what the friends have done is to continue the satanic assault on Job of which we read in chapters 1 and 2. They have broken Job down into the dust, although they thought they were helping him up. They have actually confirmed him more and more in his misery, in their inability to relate their faith in God to the depths of his need.

Yet as we read these chapters, there are times when it is hard to say of these three friends that they are getting it wrong. They are surely earnest and religious people. Their motivation is to help their friend. At certain points their words are marvellous celebrations of the majesty of God. Their falsehood, which merits God's rebuke, is not blatant evil – it is easily mistaken for good words. Is it not right to magnify the sovereign majesty and justice of God?

So how are we to understand what has gone wrong?

A clue is given to us, as we have hinted before, in the way Job responds to their speeches. He nowhere complains that they are not telling the truth. It is just that they simply do not engage with him where he is. Again and again he upbraids them for the useless-ness and the inappropriateness of their counsel.

He complains that a despairing man should have the devotion of his friends, 'But my brothers are as undependable as intermittent streams' (6:15). They have 'proved to be of no help' (6:21); they would even 'barter away' their friend (6:27). 'Doubtless', Job mocks, 'you are the people, and wisdom will die with you!' (12:2). 'But I have a mind as well as you', he argues (12:3); 'What you know, I also know; I am not inferior to you' (13:2). 'If only you would be altogether silent' (13:5); 'Keep silent and let me speak' (13:13). 'Miserable comforters are you all,' he cries (16:2); 'Will your long-winded speeches never end?' (16:3). If I were in your place, he implies, I would make sure that my words brought you comfort, encouragement and relief (16:5). 'How long will you torment me and crush me with your words?' (19:2). 'Have pity on me, my friends, have pity, for the hand of God has struck me' (19:21). In bitter and cynical reproach he calls out, 'How you have helped the powerless! How you have saved the arm that is feeble! What advice you have offered to one without wisdom! And what great insight you have displayed!' (26:2–3).

All in all, Job is fairly unimpressed.

The living God

The friends are working with a theoretical knowledge of God, a static and unchanging picture of him, which they then apply to every situation. Job, rather, is facing us with a picture of God which is dynamic and alive. We are (as Karl Barth put it) 'plunged into the strain and stress of the ongoing history of Yahweh with him'.[25] There is nothing abstract, theoretical or distant about Job's relationship with God. 'Everything he says, whether right or wrong, is baptised in the fire of a painful encounter with Him.'[26] Job is constantly struggling with his relationship with God, incomprehensible though it seems. The friends are resting in a detached theology which never actually touches Job's needs. That is what makes it into a lie. That is what brings the Lord's wrath upon them. They enclose their relationship with God within a fixed and orderly structure – God is kept within a manageable and tidy box. And yet the whole of the book of Job shatters that box, breaks open the moulds, and demands that we face God, the living God, in his appalling and frightening freedom.

The three friends got it wrong – but their wrong was 'clothed in the garb of that which is right'.[27] By so doing they did not allow space for the two crucial themes of Job's experience – the freedom of God, and the person freed by and for him.

> Yahweh as the free God of the free man Job, and Job as the free man of this free God, together in their divine and human freedom enter into the crisis in which God becomes so incomprehensible to Job even though He will not let him go, and Job becomes so angry against God even though he will not let Him go.[28]

Job takes us to the severity of God and the misery of humanity, to the silence of God and the despair of humanity, and eventually to the gracious self-revelation of God and the restoration of humanity. But this is what the friends never see or understand. Their God is safe. Job's God is frighteningly free. Their God cannot act in freedom of choice either to withhold his presence or manifest his gracious love. Job's God is alive. He is not only majestically transcendent, but intimately involved. Even when Job could feel his presence no longer, he held on in faith to the fact that God would not and could not let him go. Our next chapter will open more fully the depths of the struggle which this required.

[25] K. Barth, *Church Dogmatics*, IV/3, p. 459. [26] *Ibid.*, p. 459.
[27] *Ibid.*, p. 459. [28] *Ibid.*, p. 460.

Some implications

The error of these friends has implications for our understanding of faith. For the friends, faith was a rational system of belief, detached from the reality of a living relationship with God (Eliphaz), or a truth held on to because others said so (Bildad), or even a view of the world which fitted in with common sense (Zophar). But faith for Job is not a logical system of credal statements. Faith is a dynamic relationship with the living God, which is sustained even when God seems to have let him down. Faith for Job is the gift which God has given him to enable him to go on living in his uncertainties. Faith does not provide answers, but it is a hand in the darkness keeping alive that trust that despite all appearances, God is still on his side.

In his Christmas Broadcast on 25 December 1939, King George VI quoted these words:

And I said to the man who stood at the gate of the year: 'Give me a light that I may tread safely into the unknown'. And he replied: 'Go out into the darkness and put your hand into the hand of God. That shall be to you better than light and safer than a known way.'[29]

The error of the friends has implications also for our pastoral theology and our pastoral care. For ministry is not only about the all-important task of proclaiming the truth of the gospel; it is also about paying attention to the particular and the concrete. It is not only proclaiming the transcendence of God; it is affirming the sanctity of the ordinariness and the apparently trivial in people's lives. It is not only pointing another person to God as it were from afar, it is also sitting with him on the ash heap to listen to his real feelings and struggles, and to let our theology and our preaching and our counselling engage with him *there*.

Practical theology

It is much easier to keep our distance, like these three miserable comforters; to avoid engaging in the personally pressing questions, and to keep our theology academic. But this leaves Job in his pain. Let us learn from the inappropriateness of these three friends not only the importance of a practical theology which engages with human need, but also that to a large extent the medium is the message. In the New Testament, how frequently the divine message

[29] Quoted from the Introduction to *The Desert* by Minnie Louise Haskins.

is expressed in terms which *engage* with the concrete and particular situation of the readers. In 2 Corinthians, for example, we are not given an abstract discourse on the ministry of reconciliation, but one which arises from and is worked out in relation to the very particular needs of the church in Corinth.

And is that not the message of the incarnation of Christ itself? We preach a Christ who has come where we are, in whom, as Thomas Oden puts it, 'God assumes our frame of reference'.[30] Is the incarnation not a 'divine empathy', to use the counselling term, in which Christ engages with us in our humanity without losing his self-identity? God has come where we are, and engages with us as we are in our ordinariness, even in our trivia. The day to day of our lives matters to him. And it is not a simple matter of our getting what we deserve. God does not deal with us simply on the basis of 'you reap what you sow'. He places this theological truth within a broader context of sovereign grace, which prevents us from linking suffering to particular sins.

In the Christ who bears our judgment for us, we no longer carry the burden of our sins. In the Christ whose life is united with ours by the Holy Spirit, we are given the reward of fellowship with God. In the Christ who suffers for us on the cross, the simple law of deserts is superseded and God meets us in grace, not because we deserve it but because of his love. Within his love, the mystery of suffering will find its own purpose and power. Instead of the sterile orthodoxy of natural causes, the book of Job is pressing us to look again at the meaning of our relationship with the living God.

[30] T. Oden, *Kerygma and Counseling* (Harper & Row, 1978 ed.), p. 50.

3. Job's pilgrimage of faith
(See Job 4 – 27; 29 – 31)[1]

We know, though Job doesn't, that God is working to some divine purpose which relates to the heavenly court. Job's circumstances and experiences of suffering are in some way caught up with these secret purposes of God. But from the perspective of the ash heap on which Job has been sitting, it all seems so incongruous, so unjust, so capricious. The human situation just does not make sense. Job has feared God and turned away from evil. He is renowned as a man of piety. He has cared in an exemplary way for his family. And now he is robbed of flocks and herds and children, security and health, for no apparent reason.

The physical symptoms of his disease are increasingly terrible. He has 'painful sores from the soles of his feet to the top of his head' (2:7). These cause itching, so that Job takes 'a piece of broken pottery' to scrape himself with (2:8). His appearance is disfigured (2:12), worms get into his ulcers: 'my body is clothed with worms and scabs, my skin is broken and festering' (7:5). He has bad dreams (7:14); his face is 'red with weeping, deep shadows ring my eyes' (16:16). His breath is offensive (19:17); he loses a lot of weight: 'I am nothing but skin and bones' (19:20). His bones are very painful (30:17), and his skin 'grows black and peels' (30:30). He has a high fever (30:30).

On top of the physical misery, there has been more to contend with. He has had to face the tempting voice of his wife, however well intentioned, urging him to curse God and give up on life. He has received the no-doubt-welcome presence of his friends, suffering with him in silence. But he has burst out in chapter 3 with his despairing cry of anguish: 'Tell me why?' Now he has had to

[1] Job's speeches occur in Job 6 – 7; 9 – 10; 12 – 14; 16 – 17; 19; 21; 23 – 24; 26 – 27; and 29 – 31.

cope with his well-meaning friends trying out their theological and pastoral skills on him, most of which miss the point.

We will try to follow the steps of Job's pilgrimage, and the spiralling of his emotions as he struggles to make sense not only of his condition, but also of his faith. There are seven phases to Job's response in chapters 6 to 27, and then chapters 29 to 31 which we have called 'Job's last stand'. We turn first to chapter 6, where Job gives his initial reply to Eliphaz, and then we follow the sequence of Job's responses to the various speeches of his friends.

1. Phase I: Anger against the arrows of God (Job 6 – 7)

Job defends himself (6:1–13)

Then Job replied:

> ²*'If only my anguish could be weighed*
> *and all my misery be placed on the scales!*
> ³*It would surely outweigh the sand of the seas –*
> *no wonder my words have been impetuous.*
> ⁴*The arrows of the Almighty are in me,*
> *my spirit drinks in their poison;*
> *God's terrors are marshalled against me.*
> ⁵*Does a wild donkey bray when it has grass,*
> *or an ox bellow when it has fodder?*
> ⁶*Is tasteless food eaten without salt,*
> *or is there flavour in the white of an egg?*
> ⁷*I refuse to touch it;*
> *such food makes me ill.*
>
> ⁸*'Oh, that I might have my request,*
> *that God would grant what I hope for,*
> ⁹*that God would be willing to crush me,*
> *to let loose his hand and cut me off*
> ¹⁰*Then I would still have this consolation –*
> *my joy in unrelenting pain –*
> *that I had not denied the words of the Holy One.*
>
> ¹¹*'What strength do I have, that I should still hope?*
> *What prospects, that I should be patient?*
> ¹²*Do I have the strength of stone?*
> *Is my flesh bronze?*

¹³*Do I have any power to help myself,*
now that success has been driven from me?

Job is disappointed in his friends (6:14–30)

¹⁴*'A despairing man should have the devotion of*
his friends,
even though he forsakes the fear of the Almighty.
¹⁵*But my brothers are as undependable as intermittent*
streams,
as the streams that overflow
¹⁶*when darkened by thawing ice*
and swollen with melting snow,
¹⁷*but that cease to flow in the dry season,*
and in the heat vanish from their channels.
¹⁸*Caravans turn aside from their routes;*
they go up into the wasteland and perish.
¹⁹*The caravans of Tema look for water,*
the travelling merchants of Sheba look in hope.
²⁰*They are distressed, because they had been confident;*
they arrive there, only to be disappointed.
²¹*Now you too have proved to be of no help;*
you see something dreadful and are afraid.
²²*Have I ever said, "Give something on my behalf,*
pay a ransom for me from your wealth,
²³*deliver me from the hand of the enemy,*
ransom me from the clutches of the ruthless"?

²⁴*'Teach me, and I will be quiet;*
show me where I have been wrong.
²⁵*How painful are honest words!*
But what do your arguments prove?
²⁶*Do you mean to correct what I say,*
and treat the words of a despairing man as wind?
²⁷*You would even cast lots for the fatherless*
and barter away your friend.

²⁸*'But now be so kind as to look at me.*
Would I lie to your face?
²⁹*Relent, do not be unjust;*
reconsider, for my integrity is at stake.
³⁰*Is there any wickedness on my lips?*
Can my mouth not discern malice?

Job continues his complaint (7:1–21)

'Does not man have hard service on earth?
   Are not his days like those of a hired man?
[2]Like a slave longing for the evening shadows,
   or a hired man waiting eagerly for his wages,
[3]so I have been allotted months of futility,
   and nights of misery have been assigned to me.
[4]When I lie down I think, "How long before I get up?"
   The night drags on, and I toss till dawn.
[5]My body is clothed with worms and scabs,
   my skin is broken and festering.

[6]'My days are swifter than a weaver's shuttle,
   and they come to an end without hope.
[7]Remember, O God, that my life is but a breath;
   my eyes will never see happiness again.
[8]The eye that now sees me will see me no longer;
   you will look for me, but I will be no more.
[9]As a cloud vanishes and is gone,
   so he who goes down to the grave does not return.
[10]He will never come to his house again;
   his place will know him no more.

[11]'Therefore I will not keep silent;
   I will speak out in the anguish of my spirit,
   I will complain in the bitterness of my soul.
[12]Am I the sea, or the monster of the deep,
   that you put me under guard?
[13]When I think my bed will comfort me
   and my couch will ease my complaint,
[14]even then you frighten me with dreams
   and terrify me with visions,
[15]so that I prefer strangling and death,
   rather than this body of mine.
[16]I despise my life; I would not live for ever.
   Let me alone; my days have no meaning.

[17]'What is man that you make so much of him,
   that you give him so much attention,
[18]that you examine him every morning
   and test him every moment?
[19]Will you never look away from me,
   or let me alone even for an instant?

> ²⁰*If I have sinned, what have I done to you,*
>   *O watcher of men?*
> *Why have you made me your target?*
> *Have I become a burden to you?*
> ²¹*Why do you not pardon my offences*
>   *and forgive my sins?*
> *For I shall soon lie down in the dust;*
>   *you will search for me, but I shall be no more.'*

We find Job here in variable mood. There are the signs of depression just around the corner.

In the 1960s Dr Elisabeth Kubler-Ross established a seminar at the University of Chicago to consider the implications of terminal illness for patients and those involved in caring for them. Her book *On Death and Dying* is widely regarded as a classic, documenting as it does the progress of feelings typical of those who are facing their last illness.[2] She looks at the stages of denial and isolation, of anger, of bargaining, depression and finally acceptance. There seem to be commonly recognized patterns of reaction in the terminally ill. Colin Murray Parkes has charted similar stages in the processes of grief in his masterly work on *Bereavement*.[3] The processes of normal grief-work involve, typically, stages of numbness and shock, followed by questioning, depression, anger and, eventually, resolution. Sometimes grief can become blocked, and so become pathologically stuck, without adequate resolution. But the general phases of the processes of normal grieving are well known.

Stages of grief

Strikingly, we discover that the book of Job, written so many centuries before ours, gives very similar insights to the stages through which Job's feelings pass as he tries to handle his own losses. His loss of family, friends, health, and the sense of the presence of God, are all bereavements. We will follow his grief-work through its various phases. Job began in chapter 2 in numbed silence, a stage of shock and unbelief. For a long time he was unable to say anything. He sat in silence on the ash heap. Eventually this gave way to his lament in chapter 3. He moved to a time of questioning – searching for some meaning in his pain. Again and again he asked, 'Why?' He longed for death, and cursed the day on which he was born (3:1ff.)

[2] E. Kubler-Ross, *On Death and Dying* (Tavistock Publications, 1970).
[3] C. M. Parkes, *Bereavement* (Tavistock Publications, 1972; Pelican Books, 1975).

71

Anger

Now in chapters 6 to 7 he is getting angry: anger is often the flip side of depression, and is a frequent normal accompaniment of grief.

So where is the anger from?

In 6:4, Job is feeling a little paranoid. The world is against him. God is against him: 'The arrows of the Almighty are in me, my spirit drinks in their poison; God's terrors are marshalled against me.'

In 6:8, he reaffirms his longing for death. 'Oh, that I might have my request, that God would grant what I hope for' – that is, to be allowed to die. Here Job's focus is still on God as the source of life – and the source of his terrors. But at times, his strength is wearing thin. 'Do I have any power to help myself?' (6:13). Surely this is a testimony we will hear many times when we are in touch with people suffering in bereavement or in depression: 'I just don't have any energy any more.' So much energy goes into maintaining our defences against stress and anxiety that we get worn out.

At other times, Job musters enough courage to get angry with his friend Eliphaz. We should read 6:14 as a rebuke: 'A despairing man should have the devotion of his friends', with the implication that Eliphaz has let him down. Job then goes on (6:15–21) to describe his friends as being about as useful to him as a dry river wadi in the summer. Just when refreshment is most needed, the streams dry up. 'Now you too have proved to be of no help' (6:21).

Anger with God

Job's anger also seems to be directed towards God. He *knows* that his suffering is not related to any specific sins (6:24, 'show me where I have been wrong'). He is under what feels like the tyranny of God. He is like a slave who longs for relief from his taskmaster (7:2); he is like a weaver's shuttle, thrown to and fro in meaningless movement (7:6); he is like a mere breath, like a cloud that so quickly fades (7:7, 9). His life has become as empty as a vapour. He is on his way to the place of the dead in Sheol, where all will be rubbed out (7:9). So why should he not speak his mind?

'Therefore', he says, 'I will not keep silent; I will speak out in the anguish of my spirit' (7:11).

His speech even dares to take up the wonderful words which we find in Psalm 8 about the glory of man, and turn them into a parody: 'What is man that you make so much of him, that you give him so much attention?' (7:17).

It is all very well to speak of the glory of man! 'I despise my

life' (7:16). Why, I don't seem to be important to God any more!
Yet, if I am so insignificant, why is God expending so much energy
on me to cause me so much misery?

Once again the angry questions pour out, Why? why? why?
(7:20–21).

God had better realize his mistake, and do something about it
soon, for Job is on his way out: 'I shall soon lie down in the dust;
you will search for me, but I will be no more' (7:21). When God
comes to make amends for all this it will be too late!

So Job has the courage to get angry – to tell it how it is. He is
so overawed by what seems like the tyranny of God's injustice –
the arrows of the Almighty – that at this stage of his journey, he
sees no glimmer of hope at all.

Appropriate anger

Anger is not always inappropriate in the people of God, though
there are some Christians who think it is. Clearly the boundary
fence between anger and sin is often a fragile one,[4] and equally
clearly a distinction must be made between anger which can be put
to creative use, and hostility which is always destructive. Anger
can be used positively, for example as a signal that things are not
right in a person's relationships, if it is also giving the energy
needed to put things right. It can be appropriate for the arousal of
anger to be the right response to certain situations, particularly in
the face of injustice.

In his powerful book *The Gospel of Anger*, Alistair Campbell
suggests that:

> The task ... which faces us, if the Christian commitment to
> compassion and to justice is to be honoured in the way we act
> towards others, as individuals and as nations, is to sever the link
> between anger and destructiveness and to find ways in which
> people's powerful reactions to life's dangers around them may
> be put to the service of human wholeness.[5]

Anger, he argues, can even be a form of caring for another. The
opposite of love is not anger but hatred or indifference. Anger,
then, is sometimes appropriate if it is creative.

It is right for Job to express anger in response to innocent
suffering, in this case his own. Christians, too, need to learn how
to handle anger appropriately and not destructively.

[4] See Eph. 4:26.
[5] A. Campbell, *The Gospel of Anger* (SPCK, 1986), p. 31.

73

2. Phase II: Despair before the mightiness of God (Job 9 – 10)

Job recognizes God's justice and power (9:1–13)

Then Job replied:

> ²*'Indeed, I know that this is true.*
>   *But how can a mortal be righteous before God?*
> ³*Though one wished to dispute with him,*
>   *he could not answer him one time out of a thousand.*
> ⁴*His wisdom is profound, his power is vast.*
>   *Who has resisted him and come out unscathed?*
> ⁵*He moves mountains without their knowing it*
>   *and overturns them in his anger.*
> ⁶*He shakes the earth from its place*
>   *and makes its pillars tremble.*
> ⁷*He speaks to the sun and it does not shine;*
>   *he seals off the light of the stars.*
> ⁸*He alone stretches out the heavens*
>   *and treads on the waves of the sea.*
> ⁹*He is the Maker of the Bear and Orion,*
>   *the Pleiades and the constellations of the south.*
> ¹⁰*He performs wonders that cannot be fathomed,*
>   *miracles that cannot be counted.*
> ¹¹*When he passes me, I cannot see him;*
>   *when he goes by, I cannot perceive him.*
> ¹²*If he snatches away, who can stop him?*
>   *Who can say to him, "What are you doing?"*
> ¹³*God does not restrain his anger;*
>   *even the cohorts of Rahab cowered at his feet.*

How can Job hope to face God in court? (9:14–24)

> ¹⁴*'How then can I dispute with him?*
>   *How can I find words to argue with him?*
> ¹⁵*Though I were innocent, I could not answer him;*
>   *I could only plead with my Judge for mercy.*
> ¹⁶*Even if I summoned him and he responded,*
>   *I do not believe he would give me a hearing.*
> ¹⁷*He would crush me with a storm*
>   *and multiply my wounds for no reason.*
> ¹⁸*He would not let me regain my breath*
>   *but would overwhelm me with misery.*

^{19}*If it is a matter of strength, he is mighty!*
  And if it is a matter of justice, who will summon him?
^{20}*Even if I were innocent, my mouth would condemn me;*
  if I were blameless, it would pronounce me guilty.

^{21}'*Although I am blameless,*
  I have no concern for myself;
  I despise my own life.
^{22}*It is all the same; that is why I say,*
  "*He destroys both the blameless and the wicked.*"
^{23}*When a scourge brings sudden death,*
  he mocks the despair of the innocent.
^{24}*When a land falls into the hands of the wicked,*
  he blindfolds its judges.
  If it is not he, then who is it?

Job renews his despairing complaint (9:25–35)

^{25}'*My days are swifter than a runner;*
  they fly away without a glimpse of joy.
^{26}*They skim past like boats of papyrus,*
  like eagles swooping down on their prey.
^{27}*If I say, "I will forget my complaint,*
  I will change my expression, and smile,"
^{28}*I still dread all my sufferings,*
  for I know you will not hold me innocent.
^{29}*Since I am already found guilty,*
  why should I struggle in vain?
^{30}*Even if I washed myself with soap*
  and my hands with washing soda,
^{31}*you would plunge me into a slime pit*
  so that even my clothes would detest me.

^{32}'*He is not a man like me that I might answer him,*
  that we might confront each other in court.
^{33}*If only there were someone to arbitrate between us,*
  to lay his hand upon us both,
^{34}*someone to remove God's rod from me,*
  so that his terror would frighten me no more.
^{35}*Then I would speak up without fear of him,*
  but as it now stands with me, I cannot.

Job protests at the way God treats him (10:1–17)

'I loathe my very life;
   therefore I will give free rein to my complaint
   and speak out in the bitterness of my soul.
²I will say to God: Do not condemn me,
   but tell me what charges you have against me.
³Does it please you to oppress me,
   to spurn the work of your hands,
   while you smile on the schemes of the wicked?
⁴Do you have eyes of flesh?
   Do you see as a mortal sees?
⁵Are your days like those of a mortal
   or your years like those of a man,
⁶that you must search out my faults
   and probe after my sin –
⁷though you know that I am not guilty
   and that no-one can rescue me from your hand?

⁸'Your hands shaped me and made me.
   Will you now turn and destroy me?
⁹Remember that you moulded me like clay.
   Will you now turn me to dust again?
¹⁰Did you not pour me out like milk
   and curdle me like cheese,
¹¹clothe me with skin and flesh
   and knit me together with bones and sinews?
¹²You gave me life and showed me kindness,
   and in your providence watched over my spirit.

¹³'But this is what you concealed in your heart,
   and I know that this was in your mind:
¹⁴If I sinned, you would be watching me
   and would not let my offence go unpunished.
¹⁵If I am guilty – woe to me!
   Even if I am innocent, I cannot lift my head,
   for I am full of shame
   and drowned in my affliction.
¹⁶If I hold my head high, you stalk me like a lion
   and again display your awesome power against me.
¹⁷You bring new witnesses against me
   and increase your anger towards me;
   your forces come against me wave upon wave.

Job longs for death (10:18–22)

>   ¹⁸'*Why then did you bring me out of the womb?*
>   *I wish I had died before any eye saw me.*
>   ¹⁹*If only I had never come into being,*
>   *or had been carried straight from the womb to the grave!*
>   ²⁰*Are not my few days almost over?*
>   *Turn away from me so that I can have a moment's joy*
>   ²¹*before I go to the place of no return,*
>   *to the land of gloom and deep shadow,*
>   ²²*to the land of deepest night,*
>   *of deep shadow and disorder,*
>   *where even the light is like darkness.'*

Bildad has had his say in chapter 8, offering traditional orthodoxy of a rather dead and irrelevant sort. Now Job replies again in chapters 9 to 10, and his mood is one of despair.

God's justice and power

Job begins by picking up Bildad's reference to the justice of God (8:3) and asks, 'How can a mortal be righteous before God?' (9:2).

He goes on to speak of God's wisdom, strength, creative power, anger, commanding might, and great and marvellous deeds (9:4–10). 'His wisdom is profound, his power is vast . . . He moves mountains . . . He shakes the earth . . . He stretches out the heavens . . . He is the Maker of the Bear and Orion, the Pleiades and the constellations of the south. He performs wonders . . . miracles.' So, Job is forced to ask, How can I make any impression on a God as great and lofty as this?

'When he passes me, I cannot see him; when he goes by, I cannot perceive him' (9:11). It is all very well, Bildad, telling me all these true things about God. I believe them – but they pass me by. Why will God not make himself known to *me*, right here, now, in this misery of mine?!

Before the mightiness of God, Job can feel only despair.

Rahab

Job refers to the dragon Rahab (9:13), the name given in some ancient literature to the mythical female monster of the ocean. God's smiting Rahab is a poetic way of speaking of God's creative power, bringing order into the world by holding back the chaotic forces of the deep. (Cf. here Job 26:12, and also 38:8–11.)

But, says Job, if the dragon Rahab could not stand before God, and 'cowered at his feet' (9:13), what hope have I, when, as it were,

I face God in court? If it is a contest of strength, God will win hands down; if it is a matter of justice, God holds all the aces (9:19). So although I know I am innocent (9:15), there is nothing I can say which seems to make any difference. All I can hope for is to throw myself on God's mercy.

God seems to dispose of everyone the same way in any case (9:22) – he destroys the blameless along with the wicked – so, 'Since I am already found guilty, why should I struggle in vain?' (9:29).

Job's anger has now given way to a sense of hopelessness. In him, the longing for God, and a terror of actually meeting God are so closely woven together that Job is left in despair. God must be the author of all this suffering – so what does that do to Job's faith in God? It would be easier if he did not believe. It is Job's very faith in the ultimate goodness and justice of God which creates his dilemma.

Trapped?

This is not too far from the feelings many of us have on occasion. Whether we are having to cope with a depressive illness, or simply having a down day, there are times when God seems distant and threatening. We are trapped because we want it to be right between us and God, and yet we are terrified at God's distance. There are times when we are tempted to give up on God altogether, or believe that he must have given up on us. These themes are picked up in various of the psalms, which comfort us with their realism:

> Why are you cast down, O my soul?[6]

> O LORD, why dost thou cast me off?
> Why dost thou hide thy face from me?[7]

> I think of God, and I moan;
> I meditate, and my spirit faints. . . .
> Has God forgotten to be gracious?[8]

These are true feelings in the people of God on occasion, and need to be acknowledged and recognized. The real reassurance of the book of Job is that, despite all Job's anger, misery and despair, God commends him at the end of the story. As the book concludes, we discover that Job has not been wrong to feel this way. Nothing of his desperate questioning is held against him. God, as it were,

---

[6] Ps. 42:5, RSV. [7] Ps. 88:14, RSV. [8] Ps. 77:3, 9, RSV.

can take it. There is nothing that we can throw at him which can separate us from his love towards us in Jesus Christ. Paul says as much in Romans 8:38–39, at the end of a chapter in which he asks rhetorically, What shall we say to this? If God is for us (and he is!), who is against us?[9]

A glimpse of hope?

To return now to Job, we begin to find just a hint that even in his despair there are glimmers of hope. There is a change of tone towards the end of chapter 9. In a marvellous, piercing thrust forwards into the darkness, Job stretches out a first tentative feeler of hope. He cries out: 'If only there were someone to arbitrate between us, to lay his hand upon us both, someone to remove God's rod from me, so that his terror would frighten me no more' (9:33–34). Job wants an umpire. There must, surely, be someone who will see that justice is done?

The glimpse of hope that there must, somewhere, be an arbitrator does not last very long. In 10:1, Job reverts to a rather bitter tone: 'I will give free rein to my complaint and speak out in the bitterness of my soul.' This is not so much resentment as the misery of a bitter taste.

Job protests again at God's treatment of him. You have given me life – 'Your hands shaped me and made me' (10:8) – but why? In 10:18 we come round again to his agonized question, Why was I born? He wishes that he had died before anyone was aware of his birth. 'If only I had never come into being!' (10:19).

God the Creator at work

We need to pause here to note in passing the beautiful way in which Job describes his birth. Despite his overall despair at life, and his sense that God is actually destroying what he once made, Job's words here give a vivid description of the involvement of God in the processes of reproduction. From the earliest moments of embryonic life, right through to adulthood, Job's personal existence has been God's gift and God's concern:

> Your hands shaped me and made me. . . .
> Remember that you moulded me like clay. . . .
> Did you not pour me out like milk
>   and curdle me like cheese,
> clothe me with skin and flesh
>   and knit me together with bones and sinews?

[9] Rom. 8:31.

79

> You gave me life and showed me kindness,
>   and in your providence watched over my spirit.
>   (10:8–12)

It is clear from such paragraphs that, to the Old Testament mind, personal life began at conception. We now know that the processes of fertilization and implantation are more complicated, which leads some people to an agnosticism about *when* a human being's life is thought to begin. This is highly relevant to debates about human embryo research, and the thorny questions of abortion. But however ambiguous the processes of a new person's beginning are thought to be, it is surely obvious that every human being's life begins with the processes of fertilization, conception and implantation, even if we cannot say at any particular stage of that process, 'Now we are sure we are in the presence of a human person.' That fact alone should convince us that actions which deliberately destroy the life of the unborn, from the embryo to the foetus, can be justified only by arguments which could justify the taking of personal human life. Job thought his personal beginnings back into the processes of conception. So did the author of Psalm 139:

> For you created my inmost being;
>   you knit me together in my mother's womb.
> I praise you because I am fearfully and wonderfully made.[10]

The personal 'I' of the adult poet is continuous with the 'I' of his embryonic beginnings. The clarity with which this identity is affirmed of human beings who have 'made it', so to speak, into independent life outside the womb, should caution us against treating human life within the womb only on the basis of an agnosticism as to when fully personal life begins. We should, at the very least, give the voiceless human being in the womb the benefit of any doubt.

In the psalmist's mind, and in Job's, there was no doubt at all. God was there at his beginnings. However, even this marvel now seems to him a waste of time. Before the creative mightiness of God, all Job can feel at this stage is despair.

[10] Ps. 139:13–14.

3. Phase III: Terror at God's absence and God's presence (Job 12 – 14)

Job recognizes God's wisdom and power (12:1–25)

Then Job replied:

> ²'Doubtless you are the people,
>   and wisdom will die with you!
> ³But I have a mind as well as you;
>   I am not inferior to you.
>   Who does not know all these things?
>
> ⁴'I have become a laughing-stock to my friends,
>   though I called upon God and he answered –
>   a mere laughing-stock, though righteous and blameless!
> ⁵Men at ease have contempt for misfortune
>   as the fate of those whose feet are slipping.
> ⁶The tents of marauders are undisturbed,
>   and those who provoke God are secure –
>   those who carry their god in their hands.
>
> ⁷'But ask the animals, and they will teach you,
>   or the birds of the air, and they will tell you;
> ⁸or speak to the earth, and it will teach you,
>   or let the fish of the sea inform you.
> ⁹Which of all these does not know
>   that the hand of the LORD has done this?
> ¹⁰In his hand is the life of every creature
>   and the breath of all mankind.
> ¹¹Does not the ear test words
>   as the tongue tastes food?
> ¹²Is not wisdom found among the aged?
>   Does not long life bring understanding?
>
> ¹³'To God belong wisdom and power;
>   counsel and understanding are his.
> ¹⁴What he tears down cannot be rebuilt;
>   the man he imprisons cannot be released.
> ¹⁵If he holds back the waters, there is drought;
>   if he lets them loose, they devastate the land.
> ¹⁶To him belong strength and victory;
>   both deceived and deceiver are his.
> ¹⁷He leads counsellors away stripped

> *and makes fools of judges.*
> ¹⁸*He takes off the shackles put on by kings*
> *and ties a loincloth round their waist.*
> ¹⁹*He leads priests away stripped*
> *and overthrows men long established.*
> ²⁰*He silences the lips of trusted advisers*
> *and takes away the discernment of elders.*
> ²¹*He pours contempt on nobles*
> *and disarms the mighty.*
> ²²*He reveals the deep things of darkness*
> *and brings deep shadows into the light.*
> ²³*He makes nations great, and destroys them;*
> *he enlarges nations, and disperses them.*
> ²⁴*He deprives the leaders of the earth of their reason;*
> *he sends them wandering through a trackless waste.*
> ²⁵*They grope in darkness with no light;*
> *he makes them stagger like drunkards.*

Job is determined, despite his fear, to defend his integrity (13:1–28)

> '*My eyes have seen all this,*
> *my ears have heard and understood it.*
> ²*What you know, I also know;*
> *I am not inferior to you.*
> ³*But I desire to speak to the Almighty*
> *and to argue my case with God.*
> ⁴*You, however, smear me with lies;*
> *you are worthless physicians, all of you!*
> ⁵*If only you would be altogether silent!*
> *For you, that would be wisdom.*
> ⁶*Hear now my argument;*
> *listen to the plea of my lips.*
> ⁷*Will you speak wickedly on God's behalf?*
> *Will you speak deceitfully for him?*
> ⁸*Will you show him partiality?*
> *Will you argue the case for God?*
> ⁹*Would it turn out well if he examined you?*
> *Could you deceive him as you might deceive men?*
> ¹⁰*He would surely rebuke you*
> *if you secretly showed partiality.*
> ¹¹*Would not his splendour terrify you?*
> *Would not the dread of him fall on you?*
> ¹²*Your maxims are proverbs of ashes;*
> *your defences are defences of clay.*

¹³'Keep silent and let me speak;
    then let come to me what may.
¹⁴Why do I put myself in jeopardy
    and take my life in my hands?
¹⁵Though he slay me, yet will I hope in him;
    I will surely defend my ways to his face.
¹⁶Indeed, this will turn out for my deliverance,
    for no godless man would dare come before him!
¹⁷Listen carefully to my words;
    let your ears take in what I say.
¹⁸Now that I have prepared my case,
    I know I will be vindicated.
¹⁹Can anyone bring charges against me?
    If so, I will be silent and die.

²⁰'Only grant me these two things, O God,
    and then I will not hide from you:
²¹Withdraw your hand far from me,
    and stop frightening me with your terrors.
²²Then summon me and I will answer,
    or let me speak, and you reply.
²³How many wrongs and sins have I committed?
    Show me my offence and my sin.
²⁴Why do you hide your face
    and consider me your enemy?
²⁵Will you torment a wind-blown leaf?
    Will you chase after dry chaff?
²⁶For you write down bitter things against me
    and make me inherit the sins of my youth.
²⁷You fasten my feet in shackles;
    you keep close watch on all my paths
    by putting marks on the soles of my feet.

²⁸'So man wastes away like something rotten,
    like a garment eaten by moths.

Job laments human frailty (14:1–22)

'Man born of woman
    is of few days and full of trouble.
²He springs up like a flower and withers away;
    like a fleeting shadow, he does not endure.
³Do you fix your eye on such a one?
    Will you bring him before you for judgment?

⁴*Who can bring what is pure from the impure?*
No-one!
⁵*Man's days are determined;*
you have decreed the number of his months
and have set limits he cannot exceed.
⁶*So look away from him and let him alone,*
till he has put in his time like a hired man.

⁷'*At least there is hope for a tree:*
If it is cut down, it will sprout again,
and its new shoots will not fail.
⁸*Its roots may grow old in the ground*
and its stump die in the soil,
⁹*yet at the scent of water it will bud*
and put forth shoots like a plant.
¹⁰*But man dies and is laid low;*
he breathes his last and is no more.
¹¹*As water disappears from the sea*
or a river bed becomes parched and dry,
¹²*so man lies down and does not rise;*
till the heavens are no more, men will not awake
or be roused from their sleep.

¹³'*If only you would hide me in the grave*
and conceal me till your anger has passed!
If only you would set me a time
and then remember me!
¹⁴*If a man dies, will he live again?*
All the days of my hard service
I will wait for my renewal to come.
¹⁵*You will call and I will answer you;*
you will long for the creature your hands have made.
¹⁶*Surely then you will count my steps but not keep*
track of my sin.
¹⁷*My offences will be sealed up in a bag;*
you will cover over my sin.

¹⁸'*But as a mountain erodes and crumbles*
and as a rock is moved from its place,
¹⁹*as water wears away stones*
and torrents wash away the soil,
so you destroy man's hope.
²⁰*You overpower him once for all, and he is gone;*
you change his countenance and send him away.

> ²¹*If his sons are honoured, he does not know it;*
> *if they are brought low, he does not see it.*
> ²²*He feels but the pain of his own body*
> *and mourns only for himself.'*

Zophar has joined the conference in chapter 11 with his insolent, childish, know-all confidence. Job begins his response in chapter 12. He rejects Zophar's put-down, and asserts his own perception of the situation again. His friends are not all-knowing – Job's viewpoint must not be brushed aside so quickly.

'Doubtless you are the people' – the people who know, that is – Job bitterly remarks, 'and wisdom will die with you! But I have a mind as well' (12:1). Job's scorn at the irrelevance of his friends is coupled with the pain that he seems to have become the object of their derision. 'I have become a laughing-stock to my friends, though I called upon God and he answered – a mere laughing-stock, though righteous and blameless!' (12:4).

God's wisdom and power

In 12:13 – 13:1, Job describes the wisdom and omnipotence of God. Here is God's power that none can gainsay. In the worlds of nature, human society, religious community, national and international affairs (12:15–25), God's power can be discerned. But Job expresses this almost in terms of fatalistic despair: There is nothing about the wisdom and omnipotence of God that you can teach me, Zophar! I know that God is all-powerful – but where does that leave me now? 'My eyes have seen all this, my ears have heard and understood it. What you know, I also know' (13:1–2). But it doesn't actually help. So, Zophar, don't you come telling me to repent. I want to argue my case with God! (13:3–4).

Job knows that he is not sinless, but he is innocent of anything which might directly merit the suffering he has had to endure. These worthless physicians merely whitewash the problem (13:4). Why don't they just shut up? (13:13.)

So, in the next paragraph (13.13ff.) Job pleads with God, asking mainly for two things (13:20): 'Withdraw your hand far from me,' he cries; and 'Stop frightening me with your terrors' (13:21).

Job is concerned to be relieved of his misery, but he is even more concerned not to find himself driven from a place of trust in God to a place of terror before God. What troubles him most is that God will turn out to be a monster, and his faith will have been misplaced. Yet surely this cannot be?

'Why do you hide your face and consider me your enemy?' he prays (13:24). Job is caught up here in an anxiety state with a considerable element of paranoia. He is being persecuted. He finds God terrifying. He is on the edge of non-being, looking over into the abyss.

Dr Frank Lake, the missionary psychiatrist who founded the Clinical Theology Association, explored some of the feelings of Job at this point in his discussion of paranoia. He writes that the 'indelible sense of the persecutory nature of God's world'[11] is strong in Job. Where "being-itself" is mortally threatened, "well-being" is also lost.' He goes on to describe the sense in some people that their very being is falling into the abyss, and that persecutory anxiety and paranoia are taking over. It seems to us at such a time that all our 'rights to well-being are being unjustly withheld'. When this happens,

> There is a liability to project persecutoriness on to the environment throughout later life. When the condition of life actually becomes persecutory, as in Job's case, the whole soul is filled with an unrelieved sense of God's tyranny.[12]

Job laments human frailty

As we turn on to chapter 14 of the book of Job, we find Job musing again on the fact that God comes to him in the clothing of a destroyer. There seems to be hope for a tree – if it is cut down, it will sprout again (14:7). But there is no such hope for him. God even seems to be the one to 'destroy man's hope' (14:19).

Job is in the dark pit of despair. Now the depression is flooding over him like a dark cloud. People who have faced depressive illness know what Job means. 'He feels but the pain of his own body and mourns only for himself' (14:22). Depressed people become totally self-absorbed and cannot see beyond their own miserable predicament.

Depression is one of the worst pains a human being can face. The deep blackness over the mind and heart, the sense of personal worthlessness and hopelessness, the troubled sleep, loss of appetite, lethargy, lack of motivation, the constant uncontrolled weeping and often the desire for the release of death – these add up to an illness of the mind which at times becomes utterly unbearable.

> I have of late – but wherefore I know not – lost all my mirth, forgone all custom of exercises; and indeed it goes so heavily

[11] F. Lake, *Clinical Theology*, abridged edition (Darton, Longman & Todd, 1986), p. 116.   [12] *Ibid.*, p. 116

with my disposition that this goodly frame, the earth, seems to me a sterile promontory.[13]

Sometimes a depressive illness is related to body chemistry, and such a so-called 'endogenous' depression can often be helped by appropriate medication. Sometimes, as in Job's case, depression is a reactive condition; it is the way the mind and body respond to causes outside the person. It is a very common response to loss. There are times when depression can be the spiritual response to real moral guilt, and when the appropriate remedy is forgiveness and restoration. But this certainly was not part of the story with Job.

No wonder the good advice of his friends simply missed the mark.

Is hope still alive?

Yet Job is not quite at the bottom, for a few verses earlier, in 14:12–17, he passes through a phase when there seems to be another fleeting glimmer of hope.

The word 'until' comes more than once. Job is hanging on until things change. 'If a man dies, will he live again? . . . I will wait for my renewal to come. You will call and I will answer you: you will long for the creature your hands have made' (14:14–15). Will there be a time when God's wrath is past, when Job will be remembered, when his release will come? Will God be glad of Job's fellowship once again? Will there come such a time?

This man of faith and integrity holds on – Oh so fleetingly! – to a tiny hope; is it, perhaps, even of resurrection?

4. Phase IV: Hope of vindication begins to grow (Job 16 – 17)

Job describes his friends as 'miserable counsellors' (16:1-5)

Then Job replied:

> [2]*'I have heard many things like these;*
> *miserable comforters are you all!*
> [3]*Will your long-winded speeches never end?*
> *What ails you that you keep on arguing?*
> [4]*I also could speak like you,*
> *if you were in my place;*
> *I could make fine speeches against you*

---

[13] William Shakespeare, *Hamlet*, Act II, scene 2.

> *and shake my head at you.*
> ⁵*But my mouth would encourage you;*
>   *comfort from my lips would bring you relief.*

Job complains against God (16:6–17)

> ⁶*'Yet if I speak, my pain is not relieved;*
>   *and if I refrain, it does not go away.*
> ⁷*Surely, O God, you have worn me out;*
>   *you have devastated my entire household.*
> ⁸*You have bound me – and it has become a witness;*
>   *my gauntness rises up and testifies against me.*
> ⁹*God assails me and tears me in his anger*
>   *and gnashes his teeth at me;*
>   *my opponent fastens on me his piercing eyes.*
> ¹⁰*Men open their mouths to jeer at me;*
>   *they strike my cheek in scorn*
>   *and unite together against me.*
> ¹¹*God has turned me over to evil men*
>   *and thrown me into the clutches of the wicked*
> ¹²*All was well with me, but he shattered me;*
>   *he seized me by the neck and crushed me.*
> *He has made me his target;*
> ¹³ *his archers surround me.*
> *Without pity, he pierces my kidneys*
>   *and spills my gall on the ground.*
> ¹⁴*Again and again he bursts upon me;*
>   *he rushes at me like a warrior.*

> ¹⁵*'I have sewed sackcloth over my skin*
>   *and buried my brow in the dust.*
> ¹⁶*My face is red with weeping,*
>   *deep shadows ring my eyes;*
> ¹⁷*yet my hands have been free of violence*
>   *and my prayer is pure.*

Job appeals in hope to his 'witness' in heaven (16:18 – 17:2)

> ¹⁸*'O earth, do not cover my blood;*
>   *may my cry never be laid to rest!*
> ¹⁹*Even now my witness is in heaven;*
>   *my advocate is on high.*
> ²⁰*My intercessor is my friend*
>   *as my eyes pour out tears to God;*

²¹*on behalf of a man he pleads with God*
  as a man pleads for his friend.

²²*'Only a few years will pass*
  before I go on the journey of no return.
¹⁷:¹*My spirit is broken,*
  my days are cut short,
  the grave awaits me.
²*Surely mockers surround me;*
  my eyes must dwell on their hostility.

Job looks forward to death (17:3–16)

³*'Give me, O God, the pledge you demand.*
  Who else will put up security for me?
⁴*You have closed their minds to understanding;*
  therefore you will not let them triumph.
⁵*If a man denounces his friends for reward,*
  the eyes of his children will fail.

⁶*'God has made me a byword to everyone,*
  a man in whose face people spit.
⁷*My eyes have grown dim with grief;*
  my whole frame is but a shadow.
⁸*Upright men are appalled at this;*
  the innocent are aroused against the ungodly.
⁹*Nevertheless, the righteous will hold to their ways,*
  and those with clean hands will grow stronger.

¹⁰*'But come on, all of you, try again!*
  I will not find a wise man among you.
¹¹*My days have passed, my plans are shattered,*
  and so are the desires of my heart.
¹²*These men turn night into day;*
  in the face of darkness they say, "Light is near."
¹³*If the only home I hope for is the grave,*
  if I spread out my bed in darkness,
¹⁴*if I say to corruption, "You are my father,"*
  and to the worm, "My mother" or "My sister",
¹⁵*where then is my hope?*
  Who can see any hope for me?
¹⁶*Will it go down to the gates of death?*
  Will we descend together into the dust?'

The second cycle of speeches from the three friends, with Job's replies, begins in chapter 15 with Eliphaz. Job's answer starts in chapter 16, with much the same note as before: 'miserable comforters are you all!' (16:2).

Once again, he feels that God has worn him out (16:7). Job's innocence is again the paradox – he could understand God treating the ungodly like this – but not him! (16:11–17). His eyes are growing dim from grief (17:7), and his friends are useless counsellors (17:10). He feels for the most part left without hope (17:15).

Confidence

Yet here again, and now more strongly, tucked into the middle of this speech there is a paragraph of more confidence. The fleeting hope of resurrection which we met in chapter 14 seems to have developed now into a stronger hope of vindication – not on earth, but in heaven: 'Even now my witness is in heaven; my advocate is on high' (16:19). This must refer to God, and Job is here hinting at a theme which comes more strongly still later on, that vindication will come through a restoration of communion between God and himself. 'Give me, O God, the pledge you demand,' he says in 17:3; he calls on God to ensure that his case is heard.

The despair is now becoming more ambiguous. In relation to his friends, Job has really given them up as a lost cause. In relation to God, Job's one-track anger has given way to a two-track approach. There is still the sense of fear and injustice about the way God has treated him, but there is also this growing sense that all is not as it seems, and that one day, at another time and in another place, he will be vindicated.

This confidence takes a few knocks on the way, however, and Bildad's second speech in chapter 18 does not help.

5. Phase V: The Redeemer lives! (Job 19)

Job's patience is wearing thin (19:1–6)

Then Job replied:

> ²'How long will you torment me
>   and crush me with words?
> ³Ten times now you have reproached me;
>   shamelessly you attack me.
> ⁴If it is true that I have gone astray,
>   my error remains my concern alone.

⁵*If indeed you would exalt yourselves above me*
    and use my humiliation against me,
⁶*then know that God has wronged me*
    and drawn his net around me.

Job feels abandoned by God (19:7–12)

⁷*"Though I cry, "I've been wronged!" I get no response;*
    though I call for help, there is no justice.
⁸*He has blocked my way so that I cannot pass;*
    he has shrouded my paths in darkness.
⁹*He has stripped me of my honour*
    and removed the crown from my head.
¹⁰*He tears me down on every side till I am gone;*
    he uproots my hope like a tree.
¹¹*His anger burns against me;*
    he counts me among his enemies.
¹²*His troops advance in force;*
    they build a siege ramp against me
    and encamp around my tent.

Job appeals to his friends to have pity on him (19:13–22)

¹³*'He has alienated my brothers from me,*
    my acquaintances are completely estranged from me.
¹⁴*My kinsmen have gone away;*
    my friends have forgotten me.
¹⁵*My guests and my maidservants count me a stranger;*
    they look upon me as an alien.
¹⁶*I summon my servant, but he does not answer,*
    though I beg him with my own mouth.
¹⁷*My breath is offensive to my wife;*
    I am loathsome to my own brothers.
¹⁸*Even the little boys scorn me;*
    when I appear, they ridicule me.
¹⁹*All my intimate friends detest me;*
    those I love have turned against me.
²⁰*I am nothing but skin and bones;*
    I have escaped by only the skin of my teeth.

²¹*'Have pity on me, my friends, have pity,*
    for the hand of God has struck me.
²²*Why do you pursue me as God does?*
    Will you never get enough of my flesh?

Job is sure of his redeemer (19:23–29)

> ²³'*Oh, that my words were recorded,*
> *that they were written on a scroll,*
> ²⁴*that they were inscribed with an iron tool on lead,*
> *or engraved in rock for ever!*
> ²⁵*I know that my Redeemer lives,*
> *and that in the end he will stand upon the earth.*
> ²⁶*And after my skin has been destroyed,*
> *yet in my flesh I will see God;*
> ²⁷*I myself will see him*
> *with my own eyes – I, and not another.*
> *How my heart yearns within me!*
>
> ²⁸'*If you say, "How we will hound him,*
> *since the root of the trouble lies in him,"*
> ²⁹*you should fear the sword yourselves;*
> *for wrath will bring punishment by the sword,*
> *and then you will know that there is judgment.*'

Bildad's speech in chapter 18 plunges Job back into desperation. He begins his response with the anguished cry 'How long will you torment me?' (19:1).

By now in the story it is clear that Job has come to believe that if this is the best that God can do, he is not impressed. If God sends him friends like Bildad, who needs enemies? 'God has wronged me and drawn his net around me' (19:6). 'Though I cry, "I have been wronged!" I get no response; though I call for help, there is no justice' (19:7).

Pastor Richard Wurmbrand used to tell of his time as a prisoner of conscience in gaol under a repressive totalitarian regime. He illustrated the cry of fellow-believers, heard daily from the cells, as one or another was tortured for their faith. He threw back his hands, and threw back his head and gave a long, loud, agonized, terrifying scream.

That is Job's cry here. In terms of his sufferings, there is little more to be said. God has pulled up his hope like a tree (19:10). His family and friends have failed (19:13–14). His guests and even his servants count him as an alien (19:15). He is forsaken by God and by everyone else. He pleads only for pity: 'Have pity on me, my friends, have pity, for the hand of God has struck me' (19:21). The terror of God-forsakenness is taking hold, and the loss of those he loved (19:19) simply adds to the sense of loneliness and isolation. *But it is here, at the point of despair, at rock bottom, that Job's faith is given its highest lift so far.* For now, in those words always hard to translate, he speaks of his Redeemer. He wants some record of how he felt, so that when he is gone others will hear his side of the story.

> Oh, that my words were recorded,
>   that they were written on a scroll,
> that they were inscribed with an iron tool on lead,
>   or engraved in rock for ever!
> I know that my Redeemer lives,
>   and that in the end he will stand upon the earth.
> And after my skin has been destroyed,
>   yet in my flesh I will see God;
> I myself will see him
>   with my own eyes – I, and not another.
> How my heart yearns within me!

(19:23–27)

Now he ventures his faith in one who, beyond this earthly experience, will stand as his Redeemer.

Go'el: the Kinsman-Redeemer

The word Job uses, translated here as 'Redeemer', is the Hebrew word *go'el*. His hope now centres on a *go'el*. Frequently in the Bible, the *go'el* referred to a kinsman, sometimes next of kin, who intervened in a situation to preserve some family rights. This might be avenging the death of a murdered family member,[14] acting to redeem some person,[15] or some property.[16] It might, as in the case of the story of Ruth, involve marrying a widow to give her deceased husband an heir.[17] The *go'el* institution depends on the solidarity of the kinship group. The *go'el* is a *kinsman-redeemer*.

The word *go'el* is also used by the covenant people to refer to Yahweh, their covenant God. In the early days when God made himself known to Moses and commissioned him to negotiate with Pharaoh for the release of the Israelite slaves from Egypt, he told Moses: 'Say therefore to the people of Israel, "I am the Lord, and I will bring you out from under the burdens of the Egyptians, and I will deliver you from their bondage, and I will redeem (*g'l*) you with an outstretched arm." '[18] The Lord who redeems his people from the burden of their slavery is their Kinsman-Redeemer. The psalmist in Psalm 72 also says:

---

[14] Nu. 35:16–28. [15] Lv. 25:48–49. [16] Lv. 25:25–28. [17] Ru. 4:3–6.
[18] Ex. 6:6, RSV.

93

> From oppression and violence he redeems (*g'l*) their life;
> and precious is their blood in his sight.[19]

The saving actions of Yahweh, the Kinsman-Redeemer, flow from his love, and express the costliness of his redeeming effort ('with an outstretched arm').[20]

Surely this picture of Yahweh must have been in Job's mind when he uses this word to speak of the one on whom his hope rests. Yet the picture is one of perplexity. God, for Job, has been his enemy (16:9), his accuser and his adversary. So is it the case that the *go'el* to whom Job looks is some third party who is going to mediate between him and God? Some commentators take this view, believing that Job's view of God, and the understanding of the *go'el* we have just outlined, are incompatible. However, there is no doubt in the very next verse that Job looks forward in faith to 'seeing God'. It seems more than likely, therefore, that the *go'el* to whom he appeals is none other than Yahweh, the covenant Lord himself. The vindicator who will stand in court on Job's behalf is God himself. Perhaps it is precisely this paradox in the nature of Job's God that we are meant to see. Job's experience of God has been of one who comes to him in the clothes of an enemy. All he has seen these past days has been the dark side of God. The name Yahweh, the personal covenant name for 'the Lord' in whom Job had earlier put his faith (1:21), has not been used since chapter 2. 'Yahweh' seems to have been replaced in Job's experience by 'the Almighty'. But now, in the very teeth of divine opposition, Job holds on to what he knows of the covenant Lord. It was Yahweh who redeemed Israel from Egypt with his outstretched arm. It will be Yahweh the Kinsman-Redeemer who will vindicate him!

Vindication

God will not let him down. When all his flesh has been destroyed by these terrible boils as well as by death itself, the living God will redeem him and vindicate his cause.

'I know that my Redeemer lives.' These words, read back through the window of the cross of Calvary, have often been a source of comfort to Christian people in a time of distress. They were immortalized not only in the Prayer Book service for the Burial of the Dead, but also by Handel in the *Messiah*. Though the full Christian meaning which they hold for us today was merely a glimmer of first light before the dawn for Job, the God in whom he trusts is the God made known to us in Jesus as the Kinsman-

---

[19] Ps. 72:14, RSV.   [20] Ex. 6:6.

Redeemer and Vindicator of those who trust in him. How marvellous that Job could have said so much, knowing so little! What a rebuke to some of us, who know so much more of God than Job ever did, that we trust him so little.

Then, in chapter 20, Zophar spoils it all again for Job.

6. Phase VI: Questions of theodicy – Job criticizes God's way of governing the world (Job 21)

Job appeals to be heard (21:1–6)

Then Job replied:

> ²*'Listen carefully to my words;*
> *let this be the consolation you give me.*
> ³*Bear with me while I speak,*
> *and after I have spoken, mock on.*
>
> ⁴*'Is my complaint directed to man?*
> *Why should I not be impatient?*
> ⁵*Look at me and be astonished;*
> *clap your hand over your mouth.*
> ⁶*When I think about this, I am terrified;*
> *trembling seizes my body.*

The wicked in fact do prosper (21:7–16)

> ⁷*'Why do the wicked live on,*
> *growing old and increasing in power?*
> ⁸*They see their children established around them,*
> *their offspring before their eyes.*
> ⁹*Their homes are safe and free from fear;*
> *the rod of God is not upon them.*
> ¹⁰*Their bulls never fail to breed;*
> *their cows calve and do not miscarry.*
> ¹¹*They send forth their children as a flock;*
> *their little ones dance about.*
> ¹²*They sing to the music of tambourine and harp;*
> *they make merry to the sound of the flute.*
> ¹³*They spend their years in prosperity*
> *and go down to the grave in peace.*
> ¹⁴*Yet they say to God, "Leave us alone!*
> *We have no desire to know your ways.*

¹⁵*Who is the Almighty, that we should serve him?*
What would we gain by praying to him?"
¹⁶*But their prosperity is not in their own hands,*
so I stand aloof from the counsel of the wicked.

The wicked do not often fall, yet all will die (21:17–26)

¹⁷*'Yet how often is the lamp of the wicked snuffed out?*
How often does calamity come upon them,
the fate God allots in his anger?
¹⁸*How often are they like straw before the wind,*
like chaff swept away by a gale?
¹⁹*It is said, "God stores up a man's punishment for his*
sons."
Let him repay the man himself, so that he will know it!
²⁰*Let his own eyes see his destruction;*
let him drink of the wrath of the Almighty.
²¹*For what does he care about the family he leaves behind*
when his allotted months come to an end?

²²*'Can anyone teach knowledge to God,*
since he judges even the highest?
²³*One man dies in full vigour,*
completely secure and at ease,
²⁴*his body well nourished,*
his bones rich with marrow.
²⁵*Another man dies in bitterness of soul,*
never having enjoyed anything good.
²⁶*Side by side they lie in the dust,*
and worms cover them both.

The friends' arguments are not in line with the facts of experience (21:27–34)

²⁷*'I know full well what you are thinking,*
the schemes by which you would wrong me.
²⁸*You say, "Where now is the great man's house,*
the tents where wicked men lived?"
²⁹*Have you never questioned those who travel?*
Have you paid no regard to their accounts –
³⁰*that the evil man is spared from the day of calamity,*
that he is delivered from the day of wrath?
³¹*Who denounces his conduct to his face?*
Who repays him for what he has done?

³²*He is carried to the grave,*
and watch is kept over his tomb.
³³*The soil in the valley is sweet to him;*
all men follow after him,
and a countless throng goes before him.

³⁴*'So how can you console me with your nonsense?*
Nothing is left of your answers but falsehood!'

Job's reply to Zophar's speech in chapter 20 leaves aside the earthly focus. His friends keep on and on about his sins and the need for repentance. Job lifts the discussion on to a new plane. Now his attention is focused on God's way of governing the world.

Reconciled to this life being a life of suffering, and trusting to his vindication by his Redeemer in the end, Job now starts to talk about theodicy: that is, he tries to justify God's ways in a world of suffering and pain.

Job rejects the logic which his friends import into their theology. Job would no doubt have shared their view that God's moral universe is one in which righteousness is rewarded and wickedness punished. The friends, we recall, had pushed the logic of this to suggest that because Job was now suffering, he must have sinned. But Job's whole experience contradicts that. Not only does *he* suffer in his *innocence*, but the wicked actually have quite a good time! Chapter 21 says a lot about the prosperity of the wicked. They seem all too often to live easily and well. Their children prosper, they die in peace. They live their lives without reference to God. How can Job's friends go on about the fact that the wicked will come to nothing, when so patently they have a better life than that of many godly people? Then Job tries to let God off the hook. 'Can anyone teach knowledge to God, since he judges even in the highest?' (21:22). Whether a person lives their life with vigour and in security or with bitterness of soul, what does it matter in the end? 'Side by side they lie in the dust and worms cover them both' (21:26). So Job turns on his miserable comforters with the view that their whole approach has been based on 'falsehood' (21:34). It is just too easy to suggest that our fortune in life is directly related to our godliness. That flies in the face of the facts.

Job is moving in the direction made more explicit, as we have seen before, by the psalmist in Psalm 73, whose feet almost slipped when he saw 'the prosperity of the wicked'.[21] So many wicked people have such an easy life. Why does God allow this?

²¹ Ps. 73:3.

> Surely in vain have I kept my heart pure;
>> in vain have I washed my hands in innocence.[22]

But then comes the turning-point in the psalmist's thought:

> When I tried to understand all this,
>> it was oppressive to me
> till I entered the sanctuary of God;
>> then I understood their final destiny.[23]

Job does not quite reach such confidence, but he is clear that the simple equation made by his friends is nothing more than 'falsehood' (21:34).

Justifying God

The question of theodicy raises fundamental issues in theology. Is the world we experience the world which God originally made? In which case, we may think, he did not make a very good job of it. Or is the world fundamentally flawed and fallen, in which case how or why did God allow his good creation to be spoiled? Can we allow God off the hook by blaming the failings within the world on sin or selfishness or Satan? If we do, is this to say that God has so limited his power that he no longer has control of world events?

A further issue relates to the way we think of God's action in the world. Has God in creation simply wound the world up and left it to tick, withdrawing himself to some deistic distance, but without further direct involvement in the way the world is? Or is he the sort of God who can intervene directly into the world's day-to-day events, who is affected by what happens in the world, and who could change things if he wanted to? If so, this leaves us with the question why does God not change some of the things which, on any showing, seem to us to be evil, or pointless suffering? Or is it perhaps that God himself is part of the world process? Is all that happens to be thought of as the creative activity of God, who is intimately involved in the chances and changes of the world, but who does not 'intervene' as it were from outside, but is rather himself to be found *in* the suffering and *in* the joys?

Theological issues

The problems of evil and suffering in the world are part of these larger questions about the nature of God and the nature of

---

[22] Ps. 73:13.   [23] Ps. 73:16–17.

creation.[24] Theologians have argued about them for a long time. Irenaeus, in the second century, developed a theodicy in which he thought of human beings created in God's image, but not yet mature in the likeness of God. There is much to be done in the processes of refining us into God's likeness. This world, with all its miseries and pain, is the sphere in which God does that work of refinement. The world then is a 'vale of Soul-making' (to use John Keats' expression). Evil has to be seen as the servant of the good. By contrast with Irenaeus, Augustine, in the fourth century operated more strongly with the picture of a fallen world. The universe which God made was essentially good, and evil represents the fact that something has gone wrong. Evil is not willed and created by God, but that does not mean that it is unreal or can be disregarded. Augustine's radical view of evil leads him to an optimism, based not on a gradually improving world, but on the need for grace from God to redeem and restore.

The book of Job does not answer the questions of theodicy: it does not tell us how to justify God's ways in the face of suffering. Indeed, it does not pose these questions as theoretical ones for theological discussion. They are, rather, personally painful questions as they impinge on a man in pain. Job's problem is not so much a question of understanding on an intellectual plane, as an existential crisis in his living relationship with the living God.

As we shall see at the end of the book, Job's questions about the way God governs the world are turned back to questions to Job. Would he do things any differently? What power does Job have to control anything in the universe? Some of the questions remain unanswered, but they are placed in a context in which God, at last, makes himself personally known, and – so to speak – takes responsibility for the way he governs the world on to his own shoulders.

From our Christian perspective, too, we are still left with uncertainties about 'the problem of suffering'. It remains a problem for us precisely because it seems to call in question the goodness or the power or the wisdom of the God in whom we believe. But God comes to us in Christ, not as the last line of a logical syllogism, solving all our intellectual problems, but as a crucified man on a cross, bearing our griefs and carrying our sorrows. The questions of theodicy have to be radically rethought in the light of the crucified God.[25] We may not find answers, but we discover that in the depths of our pain and our questions, God is there beside us in the

[24] Cf. J. Hick, *Evil and the God of Love* (Macmillan, 1966).
[25] J. Moltmann, *The Crucified God* (SCM Press, 1974).

person of Christ. It is communion with him which gives us the grace to live with questions and uncertainties.

7. Phase VII: A longing for communion with God (Job 23 – 24)

Job longs for communion with God (23:1–7)

Then Job replied:

> 2'Even today my complaint is bitter;
>   his hand is heavy in spite of my groaning.
> 3If only I knew where to find him;
>   if only I could go to his dwelling!
> 4I would state my case before him
>   and fill my mouth with arguments.
> 5I would find out what he would answer me,
>   and consider what he would say.
> 6Would he oppose me with great power?
>   No, he would not press charges against me.
> 7There an upright man could present his case before him,
>   and I would be delivered for ever from my judge.

God seems inaccessible (23:8–17)

> 8'But if I go to the east, he is not there;
>   if I go to the west, I do not find him.
> 9When he is at work in the north, I do not see him;
>   when he turns to the south, I catch no glimpse of him.
> 10But he knows the way that I take;
>   when he has tested me, I shall come forth as gold.
> 11My feet have closely followed his steps;
>   I have kept to his way without turning aside.
> 12I have not departed from the commands of his lips;
>   I have treasured the words of his mouth more than
>   my daily bread.

> 13'But he stands alone, and who can oppose him?
>   He does whatever he pleases.
> 14He carries out his decree against me,
>   and many such plans he still has in store.
> 15That is why I am terrified before him;
>   when I think of all this, I fear him.

¹⁶*God has made my heart faint;*
    the Almighty has terrified me.
¹⁷*Yet I am not silenced by the darkness,*
    by the thick darkness that covers my face.

Why does God seem so inactive in the face of human wickedness? (24:1–17)

'*Why does the Almighty not set times for judgment?*
    Why must those who know him look in vain for
        such days?
²*Men move boundary stones;*
    they pasture flocks they have stolen.
³*They drive away the orphan's donkey*
    and take the widow's ox in pledge.
⁴*They thrust the needy from the path*
    and force all the poor of the land into hiding.
⁵*Like wild donkeys in the desert,*
    the poor go about their labour of foraging food;
    the wasteland provides food for their children.
⁶*They gather fodder in the fields*
    and glean in the vineyards of the wicked.
⁷*Lacking clothes, they spend the night naked;*
    they have nothing to cover themselves in the cold.
⁸*They are drenched by mountain rains*
    and hug the rocks for lack of shelter.
⁹*The fatherless child is snatched from the breast;*
    the infant of the poor is seized for a debt.
¹⁰*Lacking clothes, they go about naked;*
    they carry the sheaves, but still go hungry.
¹¹*They crush olives among the terraces;*
    they tread the winepresses, yet suffer thirst.
¹²*The groans of the dying rise from the city,*
    and the souls of the wounded cry out for help.
    But God charges no-one with wrongdoing.

¹³'*There are those who rebel against the light,*
    who do not know its ways
    or stay in its paths.
¹⁴*When daylight is gone, the murderer rises up*
    and kills the poor and needy;
    in the night he steals forth like a thief.
¹⁵*The eye of the adulterer watches for dusk;*

> *he thinks, "No eye will see me,"*
> *and he keeps his face concealed.*
> *¹⁶In the dark, men break into houses,*
> *but by day they shut themselves in;*
> *they want nothing to do with the light.*
> *¹⁷For all of them, deep darkness is their morning;*
> *they make friends with the terrors of darkness.'*

Following Eliphaz's speech in chapter 22, Job's experience moves on into a deeper phase in chapters 23 and 24. He expresses a further side to his approach to God. This is not so much now a quest for understanding as a deep yearning for fellowship from the depths of his heart. 'If only I knew where to find him,' he cries (23:3). 'If I go to the east, he is not there; if I go to the west, I do not find him. When he is at work in the north, I do not see him; when he turns to the south, I catch no glimpse of him' (23:8–9).

Job knows in his heart that his problem will be relieved not by theological dispute, nor by penitence for sins which he has not committed, nor by pulling his socks up, *but by the gift of communion with God*. It is *this* on which he now rests his hope.

In terms of present experience, God seems so inaccessible, yet the depths of faith are seen in all their glory in 23:10: 'But he knows the way that I take; when he has tested me, I shall come forth as gold.' Though God terrifies me, he says (23:16), I have kept my integrity (26:11), and I shall come forth as gold. Life can begin again! Then Job begins his puzzling again in chapter 24, asking why God seems so indifferent to the wicked. They seem to get away with anything, and God does not punish them.

Job 24:2–16 lists a variety of wrongdoings in Job's world, most of them sins against which other parts of the Old Testament are very severe; verses 1 and 17 complain that God seems to be doing nothing about them. Once again Job is puzzled by God's apparent injustice.

The next section of text presents a problem. At first sight, Job 24:18–25 seems to say almost the opposite of the previous part of the chapter, and does not seem to fit in with the rest of Job's speech. This has led some commentators to suggest that these verses really come from either Bildad or Zophar. On the other hand, perhaps Job is giving voice to his confusion: one minute he thinks that the wicked are getting off too lightly, and now he remembers that they too, like he himself, are subject to the rule of death. Either way, this poem is a mournful lament on the frailty and frustration of life:

¹⁸'*Yet they are foam on the surface of the water;*
their portion of the land is cursed,
so that no-one goes to the vineyards.
¹⁹*As heat and drought snatch away the melted snow,*
so the grave snatches away those who have sinned.
²⁰*The womb forgets them,*
the worm feasts on them;
evil men are no longer remembered
but are broken like a tree.
²¹*They prey on the barren and childless woman,*
and to the widow show no kindness.
²²*But God drags away the mighty by his power;*
though they become established, they have no assurance
of life.
²³*He may let them rest in a feeling of security,*
but his eyes are on their ways.
²⁴*For a little while they are exalted, and then they are gone;*
they are brought low and gathered up like all others;
they are cut off like ears of corn.

²⁵'*If this is not so, who can prove me false*
and reduce my words to nothing?'

(24:18–25)

8. Job 26 – 27

The muddled order of chapters 26 and 27, part of which again
some commentators allocate to Bildad and Zophar, leaves much
that is unclear, but Job has one final angry, defiant fling against his
friends at the beginning of chapter 27:

And Job continued his discourse:

²'*As surely as God lives, who has denied me justice,*
the Almighty, who has made me taste bitterness of soul,
³*as long as I have life within me,*
the breath of God in my nostrils,
⁴*my lips will not speak wickedness,*
and my tongue will utter no deceit.
⁵*I will never admit you are in the right;*
till I die, I will not deny my integrity.
⁶*I will maintain my righteousness and never let go of it;*
my conscience will not reproach me as long as I live.'

(27:1–6)

103

'My conscience remains clear,' Job can say.

Conscience

Conscience is not always a reliable guide to truth, and we have a responsibility to educate our consciences in line with the objective truth, revealed to us by God. But conscience must not be set aside. It is that 'sentiment of the understanding or perception of the heart' (as the eighteenth-century theologian Bishop Butler put it)[26] by which the voice of God can be heard in our inner beings. As Dietrich Bonhoeffer, the great German theologian who was hanged by the Nazis in 1945, wrote:

> Conscience comes from a depth which lies beyond a man's own will and reason, and it makes itself heard as the call of human existence to unity with itself. Conscience comes as an indictment of the loss of this unity and as a warning against the loss of one's self.[27]

For the Christian, that call to integrity and personal unity is the call to be centred on the being of God in Jesus Christ.

That is not to say that every voice in our inner beings is necessarily God's voice. It was possible for the National Socialists of Nazi Germany to say, 'My conscience is Adolf Hitler.' To quote Bonhoeffer again:

> When Christ, true God and true man, has become the point of unity of my existence, conscience will indeed still formally be the call of my actual being to unity with myself, but this unity . . . must be realised in fellowship with Jesus Christ.[28]

Then in conscious opposition to the National Socialists, he says, 'Jesus Christ has become my conscience.'[29]

So conscience must be trained. The Christian conscience must be educated to hear the call to personal integrity as the call to fellowship with Jesus Christ. But though conscience must be trained, it may not be ignored.

Job in conscience maintains his integrity. He was learning to hear the call to integrity in his own self as the call to deeper communion with God. To deny it would be to deny his very being.

---

[26] Joseph Butler, in 'Dissertation upon the Nature of Virtue', an appendix to his *Analogy of Religion* (1736).
[27] D. Bonhoeffer, *Ethics* (SCM Press, 1971), p. 211.   [28] *Ibid.*, p. 212.
[29] *Ibid.*, p. 212.

9. Job's pilgrimage

Now the three friends' speeches are over. Eliphaz, Bildad and Zophar have had their say. Job has responded – not answering all their points directly (because he feels they are so far off the mark), but making his own case.

We have followed him through the seven phases of his grief. After the time of numbed shock and silence, followed by his lament, longing and questioning in chapters 2 and 3, we began in chapter 4 with his anger against God, and his refusal to accept things the way they are. Angry questions in the face of God's arrows gave way in chapters 9 to 10 to despair in the face of God's almightiness. Chapters 12 to 14 showed us Job in terror, both at God's apparent absence and at his threatening presence, as Job gave way to anxiety and paranoia. Throughout these chapters there were the beginnings of a glimmer of hope, and this hope began to grow in chapters 16 to 17, only to be dashed again. The hope grew to its high point in chapter 19 with the reaching out towards the Kinsman-Redeemer who, Job believed, would one day vindicate his cause. Job then moved into a time of questioning the way God rules the world, and he opened up for us issues of theodicy: How do we make sense of God's ordering of the world in the face of so much inexplicable suffering?

Finally, Job looked forward longingly towards the time when his communion with God would be restored. There would be a resolution of grief, when life could begin again, when normality could be restored, perhaps even when, from a different perspective, some meaning could be given to the pain through which Job had passed.

Some implications

Let us pause here at some of the implications of this pilgrimage. Although it offers us no answers to our searching questions about suffering in the world, it shows us a person who is beginning to find a way of coping with them. He has not hidden his feelings. One of the strengths of the book of Job is the honest way in which Job expresses his deepest hurts and deepest longings. By the time we reach the end of the book, we will have heard the Lord himself speak from the whirlwind, and we will have a further perspective on the struggles of faith through which Job has passed. But even now we are beginning to see that we need to understand them in terms of a journey of faith. Things do not become clear all at once. At different times on his pilgrimage, he is learning different things about the ways of God. At times God seems altogether absent. At other times God seems dressed in the clothes of an enemy. Job has to work at his grief, and it takes time. There is a process to go through – it doesn't happen all at once. The spiral of grief sometimes twists round and round.

A spiral of emotion indeed it is. People who have read C. S. Lewis' *A Grief Observed* will recognize the match between Job's experience and the experience of bereavement that Lewis describes:

> Tonight all the hells of young grief have opened again; the mad words, the bitter resentment, the fluttering in the stomach, the nightmare unreality, the wallowed-in tears. For in grief, nothing 'stays put'. One keeps on emerging from a phase, but it always recurs. Round and round. Everything repeats. Am I going in circles, or dare I hope I am on a spiral?
>
> But if a spiral, am I going up or down it?[30]

But the heart of Job's problem is not only his bereavement through loss of property or family or health. It is not only the pain of illness or the frustration he feels about his friends. His problem is with God. Why has God abandoned him? Why is God far from him? Why will God not answer his prayer?

The beginnings of hope

It is here, in the questions and in the despair, that we find the seeds of hope. Through these chapters, as we have seen, a hope begins to grow, which culminates in the faith that communion between Job and God will one day be restored. There will be an umpire 'to arbitrate between us' (9:33), he says. And not only an umpire, a witness (16:19). And not only a witness but a *go'el*, a Kinsman-Redeemer who will vindicate him (19:25). God himself will take his side and all will one day be well. He may not see his vindication this side of the grave, but his hope is ultimately in God.

10. Job's last stand (Job 29 – 31)

We will pass over chapter 28 for the present, and for reasons which will become clear we will return to it in the next chapter. We turn now to chapters 29 to 31, in which Job makes his final long speech on his own behalf. This is Job's last stand. This is his last solo performance before Elihu's surprising interruption, and God's own voice from the whirlwind.

---

[30] C. S. Lewis, *A Grief Observed*, p. 46.

Job looks back on past happiness (29:1–25)

Job continued his discourse:

> ²'How I long for the months gone by,
>   for the days when God watched over me,
> ³when his lamp shone upon my head
>   and by his light I walked through darkness!
> ⁴Oh, for the days when I was in my prime,
>   when God's intimate friendship blessed my house,
> ⁵when the Almighty was still with me
>   and my children were around me,
> ⁶when my path was drenched with cream
>   and the rock poured out for me streams of olive oil.
>
> ⁷'When I went to the gate of the city
>   and took my seat in the public square,
> ⁸the young men saw me and stepped aside
>   and the old men rose to their feet;
> ⁹the chief men refrained from speaking
>   and covered their mouths with their hands;
> ¹⁰the voices of the nobles were hushed,
>   and their tongues stuck to the roof of their mouths.
> ¹¹Whoever heard me spoke well of me,
>   and those who saw me commended me,
> ¹²because I rescued the poor who cried for help,
>   and the fatherless who had none to assist him.
> ¹³The man who was dying blessed me;
>   I made the widow's heart sing.
> ¹⁴I put on righteousness as my clothing;
>   justice was my robe and my turban.
> ¹⁵I was eyes to the blind
>   and feet to the lame.
> ¹⁶I was a father to the needy;
>   I took up the case of the stranger.
> ¹⁷I broke the fangs of the wicked
>   and snatched the victims from their teeth.
>
> ¹⁸'I thought, "I shall die in my own house,
>   my days as numerous as the grains of sand.
> ¹⁹My roots will reach to the water,
>   and the dew will lie all night on my branches.
> ²⁰My glory will remain fresh in me,
>   the bow ever new in my hand."

²¹'Men listened to me expectantly,
    waiting in silence for my counsel.
²²After I had spoken, they spoke no more;
    my words fell gently on their ears.
²³They waited for me as for showers
    and drank in my words as the spring rain.
²⁴When I smiled at them, they scarcely believed it;
    the light of my face was precious to them.
²⁵I chose the way for them and sat as their chief;
    I dwelt as a king among his troops;
    I was like one who comforts mourners.

Job bewails his present misery (30:1–31)

'But now they mock me, men younger than I,
    whose fathers I would have disdained to put with my
        sheep dogs.
²Of what use was the strength of their hands to me,
    since their vigour had gone from them?
³Haggard from want and hunger,
    they roamed the parched land
    in desolate wastelands at night.
⁴In the brush they gathered salt herbs,
    and their food was the root of the broom tree.
⁵They were banished from their fellow-men,
    shouted at as if they were thieves.
⁶They were forced to live in the dry stream beds,
    among the rocks and in holes in the ground.
⁷They brayed among the bushes
    and huddled in the undergrowth.
⁸A base and nameless brood,
    they were driven out of the land.

⁹'And now their sons mock me in song;
    I have become a byword among them.
¹⁰They detest me and keep their distance;
    they do not hesitate to spit in my face.
¹¹Now that God has unstrung my bow and afflicted me,
    they throw off restraint in my presence.
¹²On my right the tribe attacks;
    they lay snares for my feet,
    they build their siege ramps against me.
¹³They break up my road;
    they succeed in destroying me –

without anyone's helping them.
¹⁴*They advance as through a gaping breach;*
amid the ruins they come rolling in.
¹⁵*Terrors overwhelm me;*
my dignity is driven away as by the wind,
my safety vanishes like a cloud.

¹⁶*'And now my life ebbs away;*
days of suffering grip me.
¹⁷*Night pierces my bones;*
my gnawing pains never rest.
¹⁸*In his great power God becomes like clothing to me;*
he binds me like the neck of my garment.
¹⁹*He throws me into the mud,*
and I am reduced to dust and ashes.

²⁰*'I cry out to you, O God, but you do not answer;*
I stand up, but you merely look at me.
²¹*You turn on me ruthlessly;*
with the might of your hand you attack me.
²²*You snatch me up and drive me before the wind;*
you toss me about in the storm.
²³*I know you will bring me down to death,*
to the place appointed for all the living.

²⁴*'Surely no-one lays a hand on a broken man*
when he cries for help in his distress.
²⁵*Have I not wept for those in trouble?*
Has not my soul grieved for the poor?
²⁶*Yet when I hoped for good, evil came;*
when I looked for light, then came darkness.
²⁷*The churning inside me never stops;*
days of suffering confront me.
²⁸*I go about blackened, but not by the sun;*
I stand up in the assembly and cry for help.
²⁹*I have become a brother of jackals,*
a companion of owls.
³⁰*My skin grows black and peels;*
my body burns with fever.
³¹*My harp is tuned to mourning,*
and my flute to the sound of wailing.

Job asserts his integrity, as in a court of law (31:1–40)

'I made a covenant with my eyes
    not to look lustfully at a girl.
²For what is man's lot from God above,
    his heritage from the Almighty on high?
³Is it not ruin for the wicked,
    disaster for those who do wrong?
⁴Does he not see my ways
    and count my every step?

⁵'If I have walked in falsehood
    or my foot has hurried after deceit –
⁶let God weigh me in honest scales
    and he will know that I am blameless –
⁷if my steps have turned from the path,
    if my heart has been led by my eyes,
    or if my hands have been defiled,
⁸then may others eat what I have sown,
    and may my crops be uprooted.

⁹'If my heart has been enticed by a woman,
    or if I have lurked at my neighbour's door,
¹⁰then may my wife grind another man's grain,
    and may other men sleep with her.
¹¹For that would have been shameful,
    a sin to be judged.
¹²It is a fire that burns to Destruction;
    it would have uprooted my harvest.

¹³'If I have denied justice to my menservants and
        maidservants
    when they had a grievance against me,
¹⁴what will I do when God confronts me?
    What will I answer when called to account?
¹⁵Did not he who made me in the womb make them?
    Did not the same one form us both within our mothers?

¹⁶'If I have denied the desires of the poor
    or let the eyes of the widow grow weary,
¹⁷if I have kept my bread to myself,
    not sharing it with the fatherless –
¹⁸but from my youth I reared him as would a father,
    and from my birth I guided the widow –

¹⁹*if I have seen anyone perishing for lack of clothing,*
or a needy man without a garment,
²⁰*and his heart did not bless me*
for warming him with the fleece from my sheep,
²¹*if I have raised my hand against the fatherless,*
knowing that I had influence in court,
²²*then let my arm fall from the shoulder,*
let it be broken off at the joint.
²³*For I dreaded destruction from God,*
and for fear of his splendour I could not do such things.

²⁴*'If I have put my trust in gold*
or said to pure gold, "You are my security,"
²⁵*if I have rejoiced over my great wealth,*
the fortune my hands had gained,
²⁶*if I have regarded the sun in its radiance*
or the moon moving in splendour,
²⁷*so that my heart was secretly enticed*
and my hand offered them a kiss of homage,
²⁸*then these also would be sins to be judged,*
for I would have been unfaithful to God on high.

²⁹*'If I have rejoiced at my enemy's misfortune*
or gloated over the trouble that came to him –
³⁰*I have not allowed my mouth to sin*
by invoking a curse against his life –
³¹*if the men of my household have never said,*
"Who has not had his fill of Job's meat?" –
³²*but no stranger had to spend the night in the street,*
for my door was always open to the traveller –
³³*if I have concealed my sin as men do,*
by hiding my guilt in my heart
³⁴*because I so feared the crowd*
and so dreaded the contempt of the clans
that I kept silent and would not go outside –

³⁵*('Oh, that I had someone to hear me!*
I sign now my defence – let the Almighty answer me;
let my accuser put his indictment in writing.
³⁶*Surely I would wear it on my shoulder,*
I would put it on like a crown.
³⁷*I would give him an account of my every step;*
like a prince I would approach him.) –

> ³⁸'*if my land cries out against me*
> *and all its furrows are wet with tears,*
> ³⁹*if I have devoured its yield without payment*
> *or broken the spirit of its tenants,*
> ⁴⁰*then let briers come up instead of wheat*
> *and weeds instead of barley.'*

The words of Job are ended.

Job begins by saying in effect that there is nothing more to be said.

Job looks back

In 29:1, we again get the introductory formula 'Job continued his discourse'. Job is yearning for that sense of the immediacy of God's presence that he had known before. In the words of William Cowper:

> Where is the blessedness I knew
> When first I saw the Lord? . . .
>
> What peaceful hours I once enjoyed!
> How sweet their memory still!
> But they have left an aching void
> The world can never fill.³¹

Job recalls those earlier days. If only it were like that again! 'How I long for the months gone by, for the days when God watched over me, when his lamp shone upon my head and by his light I walked through darkness!' (29:2–3). Verses 2 to 11 are a longing for those earlier days, full of wistfulness and sadness. Then, in verse 11, Job's fire returns just a little: I used to be good! He recalls how he helped the poor and the fatherless, the dying man and the widow. He cared for the blind and the lame, the needy and the stranger. He has looked forward to his death with peaceful thoughts. Verses 21 to 25 recall how he was respected in the community, and how he dwelt as a king among his troops. Job really had been a very great man. 'But now they mock me, men younger than I, whose fathers I would have disdained to put with my sheep dogs' (30:1).

Job's present misery

In 30:1–8, Job reminds himself how people make fun of him. 'I

---

³¹ William Cowper, 'O for a closer walk with God'.

have become a byword' (30:9) because 'God has unstrung my bow and afflicted me' (30:11).

Now . . . now it is so different.

In 30:16–19, Job catalogues his feelings: life ebbs away, suffering grips him, his bones are pierced, his gnawing pains never rest; he is thrown into the mud and reduced to dust and ashes.

The silence of God is the hardest of all. 'I cry out to you, O God, but you do not answer' (30:20). That is the hardest cruelty – what seems to be the cruelty of God.

Job expresses the depths to which he has been driven: 'When I hoped for good, evil came; when I looked for light, then came darkness. The churning inside me never stops; days of suffering confront me' (30:26–27).

Then, with clenched fist shaken to heaven and to earth, he holds up his head once more like a prince, and insists on his innocence.

Job asserts his integrity

Chapter 31 is set out like a legal oath. The oath formula comes again and again: 'If I have . . . then . . .' In terms of purity (31:1), truth (31:5), honour (31:13–14), justice (31:16–17), moral priorities (31:24–28), neighbour love (31:29–30) – I have done it right! THIS IS MY SIGNATURE: LET THE ALMIGHTY ANSWER ME! (31:35).

What courage! What integrity! What faith in God – to risk challenging God like this! Even if he is going to have to learn that he is speaking out of ignorance of the ways of God, we cannot but admire his trust; he knows that God can take it – so he throws it all on God. Always, throughout, Job's face is turned towards God.

> Oh, that I had someone to hear me!
>> I sign now my defence – let the Almighty answer me;
>> let my accuser put his indictment in writing.
> Surely I would wear it on my shoulder.
>> I would put it on like a crown.
> I would give him an account of my every step;
>> like a prince I would approach him.
>
> (31:35–37)

If God will come and answer for what he has done, I will meet him like a prince. I take my stand on the justice and goodness of God.

Job is here, ironically, challenging God to do what – all unbeknown to Job – God had challenged Satan to do at the beginning: to say what is the fault with Job.

113

Within the purposes of God

These powerful chapters of Job's pilgrimage not only give us a deep insight into the psychology of grief; they open up for us a pilgrimage of faith which is marked more than anything else by Job's integrity. We may feel he indulges at times in self-pity. We may feel he becomes too self-assertive in places. But we cannot mistake his integrity. These chapters tell us that good and innocent people do suffer in this world. They tell us that the way Eliphaz, Bildad and Zophar pressed the logic of the doctrine of rewards, so as to make it a matter of simple cause and effect, grievously misses the mark. They show us the misery caused by inappropriate pastoral application even of the truth. These chapters tell us that the people God has made have a rightful place in the Creator's purposes, and that if God is a God of power and of goodness, then surely communion between human beings and God is possible. That is the hope. They give us a glimpse of life beyond Sheol, and a hint that Job is beginning to realize that there is more to his story than meets the eye. For as we know, he is the Lord's servant, and as we also know, it is through the suffering of the servant of God that God's purposes of grace are achieved.

Job, in his freedom to receive both good and bad from God, as the Suffering Servant of the Lord, through whom God is working out his purposes, stands for us as a type of Jesus Christ. Jesus Christ is the true Servant, the true Witness, whose reality shines out through the life of this man from Uz. Job, in his obedience, is a witness to this True Witness. The God who is free both to give and to take away (1:21), is the God who gives Job his freedom to experience this freedom of God. The relationship, despite all appearances so far, is one of grace. Job will discover this for himself in due course.

There are times when we come into touch with those who are 'going through it'. May God give us grace to hold out these two positive strands: *hope* in the place of despair, based on *communion* in the place of alienation. For though Job does not yet know this, God himself is present with Job both in his despair, and in his alienation. God has never let go of his hand.

Thielicke catches the theme in his masterly way:

This is the holy God for whom our lost lives are an unspeakable hurt, and who nevertheless says Yes to us . . . God himself suffers there where the Crucified hangs. That is what all this means. When he cries 'My God, my God, why hast thou forsaken me?' the eternal heart abandons itself to all the forsakenness and despair that a man suffers in his separation from God. Nothing more stands between God and me, because he has become my brother. At the bottom of every abyss he stands beside me.[32]

That is something Job has yet to discover.

As we move on in the book of Job, Elihu will bring us a different perspective – preparing us, to some extent at least, for the climax of the book. For eventually God himself does come to Job, but in a way and with a word that Job – and we, the readers – certainly do not expect.

[32] Thielicke, *I Believe*, p. 117.

4. Wisdom: human and divine (Job 28; 32 – 37)

It may be that by now we feel the need of a break from the intensity of Job's anguish. The author has sustained about thirty chapters of the most harrowing dialogue leading to Job's passionate avowal of his innocence. Everyone, including ourselves the readers, is exhausted.

Ready for a change

We are ready for a change of key, a change of tempo. We are perhaps tired of the to-ing and fro-ing of Job and his friends. They do not engage with each other. They only frustrate each other. The friends have been trying to justify God to Job by insisting on his sinfulness, and they have set themselves to prove that Job is in the wrong. Job has tried to justify himself to his friends by insisting that God has treated him unjustly: he has to prove that God is in the wrong. There is an increasing intemperateness in Job's responses, as he believes, rightly, that his friends have completely misrepresented his position. They have not engaged with him at all. They have not met him in his pain. There is also a growing intemperateness in the friends' responses to Job, as they believe – and they may be right – that Job has overstepped the mark in his view of God, and said things that no pious believer should say.

Perhaps the time has come for some objective reflection. Perhaps we now need to stand back from this unseemly debate and think clearly. Perhaps we need a critique of both Job and his friends from the perspective of a dispassionate observer, to pause and reflect on what has been happening.

The text provides us with breathing spaces in two ways. First, chapter 28, which we passed over earlier, stands as a sort of intrusion into the cycles of speeches. It separates the dialogue between Job and the three friends from what we called 'Job's last

stand'. It is a marvellous Hymn to Wisdom. Secondly, chapters 32
to 37 introduce us to a new contributor who has not spoken before:
Elihu. He gives us an occasion to pause and take stock. He also
has things to say about wisdom.

Let us begin in Job 28.

1. Hymn to Wisdom (Job 28)

> 'There is a mine for silver
> and a place where gold is refined.
> [2]Iron is taken from the earth,
> and copper is smelted from ore.
> [3]Man puts an end to the darkness;
> he searches the farthest recesses
> for ore in the blackest darkness.
> [4]Far from where people dwell he cuts a shaft,
> in places forgotten by the foot of man;
> far from men he dangles and sways.
> [5]The earth, from which food comes,
> is transformed below as by fire;
> [6]sapphires come from its rocks,
> and its dust contains nuggets of gold.
> [7]No bird of prey knows that hidden path,
> no falcon's eye has seen it.
> [8]Proud beasts do not set foot on it,
> and no lion prowls there.
> [9]Man's hand assaults the flinty rock
> and lays bare the roots of the mountains.
> [10]He tunnels through the rock;
> his eyes see all its treasures.
> [11]He searches the sources of the rivers
> and brings hidden things to light.
>
> [12]'But where can wisdom be found?
> Where does understanding dwell?
> [13]Man does not comprehend its worth;
> it cannot be found in the land of the living.
> [14]The deep says, "It is not in me",
> the sea says, "It is not with me."
> [15]It cannot be bought with the finest gold,
> nor can its price be weighed in silver.
> [16]It cannot be bought with the gold of Ophir,
> with precious onyx or sapphires.

117

17Neither gold nor crystal can compare with it,
nor can it be had for jewels of gold.
18Coral and jasper are not worthy of mention;
the price of wisdom is beyond rubies.
19The topaz of Cush cannot compare with it:
it cannot be bought with pure gold.

20'Where then does wisdom come from?
Where does understanding dwell?
21It is hidden from the eyes of every living thing,
concealed even from the birds of the air.
22Destruction and Death say,
"Only a rumour of it has reached our ears."
23God understands the way to it
and he alone knows where it dwells,
24for he views the ends of the earth
and sees everything under the heavens.
25When he established the force of the wind
and measured out the waters,
26when he made a decree for the rain
and a path for the thunderstorm,
27then he looked at wisdom and appraised it;
he confirmed it and tested it.
28And he said to man,
"The fear of the Lord – that is wisdom,
and to shun evil is understanding." '

Job 28 is about Wisdom, human and divine. Many commentators regard this chapter as an addition to the flow of the text. Others see it as fulfilling a function rather like the chorus of a Greek drama – an opportunity to stand back and reflect how far we have come and how far there is still to go. Yet others understand the chapter as integral to a long speech of Job which runs from chapter 26 to chapter 31. On this third view, the theme of wisdom which we find in 26:3 ('What advice you have offered to one without wisdom!') and in 26:12, is picked up and explored more fully and more theologically in chapter 28, with chapter 27 coming in between as Job's own personal commitment to the life which pleases God. The approach taken in this book follows the second of these views, namely that the author of the book of Job has included in chapter 28 certain crucial insights of his own, to help us stand back reflectively to attempt to understand something of the book's purpose. Its theme, as we said, is Wisdom.

The ability to cope

We need to remind ourselves that one aspect of human wisdom is, as Eric Heaton put it, 'the ability to cope'.[1] There are in the Wisdom tradition (that style of literature of Old Testament times which is illustrated in our Bibles by books such as Proverbs and Ecclesiastes, as well as by Job) three strands to human wisdom. There is, first, the proverbial wisdom of the Wisdom schools – the commonsense utterances about life and behaviour, passed on from fathers to sons, teachers to pupils. This wisdom, seen for example in the book of Proverbs, is a sort of commonsense morality. Secondly, there is the sort of wisdom seen in Ecclesiastes – the scribal skills of intellectual exploration; the searching for answers to the riddles of life. Thirdly, there is human wisdom, illustrated most clearly here in Job 28 in the writer's admiration for science and technology, especially the skill of the mining industry. In each case human wisdom is demonstrated in an ability to cope – to cope with the ordinary demands of day-to-day morality; to cope with knowing what to do, how to govern, how to rule; to cope with the raw materials of the craftsmen's skills.

But in every sphere, true wisdom depends on obedience to God, and not on natural or theoretical knowledge.

Job 28

This is the significance of Job 28. In a poem of great beauty, the author admires first the skill of the miner. Verses 1 to 6 refer to the refining of silver and gold, the digging of iron ore, the smelting of copper, the mining of sapphires. 'Man . . . searches the farthest recesses for ore in the blackest darkness' (28:3). Perhaps there is more than a hint here that even the darkness of Job's life may yet yield its treasures.

The author goes on to illustrate in verses 7 to 8 how this human skill surpasses that of birds and animals. Even the keen sight of the falcon and the courage of the lion fail to match the skill of the miner, digging treasures from the depths. He then extols the extent of human power and might, mentioning human skill at the rock face, in the mountains, under the ground, and in the rivers (28:9–11). Throughout the natural world, human skill is seen, and is to be applauded.

Then, in comparison with this, he reflects on what might almost be the main theological question of the book of Job: 'But where can wisdom be found? Where does understanding dwell?' (28:12).

[1] Heaton, p. 165.

There is something more to wisdom than even the remarkable skill of the miner, the technologist, the scientific explorer. There is something that even human beings themselves do not understand. There is, we shall learn, a divine wisdom as well as human wisdom.

Mankind does not comprehend its worth (28:13). The deep powers of creation do not know (28:14). Divine wisdom is not the result of technological skill; it cannot be bought or exchanged (28:15).

True wisdom

The answer to the question as to where true wisdom is to be found escapes human beings, for true wisdom is not of this world. 'It is hidden from the eyes of every living thing, concealed even from the birds of the air. Destruction and Death say, "Only a rumour of it has reached our ears" ' (28:21–22). The truth is that only God knows the way to wisdom (28:23), for he sees everything under the heavens. It stems from his creative power (28:25–27). The fear of the Lord – life lived in communion with the Lord and in obedience to his will – is the beginning of wisdom (28:28). That is the gift which enables us to cope.

True wisdom thus remains the gift of God – and it is a gift of grace. All other skills – even the marvels of the mine, to say nothing of the orthodoxy of Bildad, the theology we shall find in Elihu, or even the innocent, upright character of Job himself – these skills are as nothing without the fear of the Lord. Wisdom is a way of living before God.

Gerhardt von Rad writes: 'The thesis that all human knowledge comes back to the question about commitment to God is a statement of penetrating perspicacity . . . One becomes competent and expert as far as the orders in life are concerned only if one begins from knowledge about God.'[2]

The divine perspective

So what does this say to Job? It reminds him – and especially reminds us, the readers, as we wrestle with Job in his pain, and struggle to make sense of his apalling situation – that there is more to life than we can understand with our senses. There is more to wisdom than even the greatest of human skills. There is a different way of looking at everything – from the perspective of God the Creator. He sees 'everything under the heavens', whereas we see only a part. There is more to Job's predicament than Job himself will ever know (though we were let in to part of the divine secret

[2] G. von Rad, *Wisdom in Israel* (SCM Press, 1972), p. 67.

in chapters 1 and 2). What is needed is a new beginning to our knowledge – to start not from our experience of misery like Job, nor from our own mystical experience like Eliphaz, not from our understanding of theological tradition like Bildad, nor from our own inflated common sense like Zophar.

True wisdom is accessible to God alone – which means that it can come from him alone. The wisdom which will contain an answer to Job can come only from God. Chapter 28 thus stands in the book of Job as a warning that any further speculations along the lines of the three friends will be fruitless. The way out of the impasse will not be from below, upwards, but from above, downwards. It will not come as part of the belief system of man-kind, but only as a gift of God. The starting-point for true knowledge of God is God himself in his own self-disclosure. We need to meet the Lord as he comes to us in grace. We need to begin with the fear of the Lord, in communion with him as he chooses to make himself known.

2. The Elihu interlude (Job 32 – 37)

(The full biblical text of the Elihu speeches in Job 32 to 37 is printed on pp. 179–188 of the Appendix.)

After Job's last stand, the three friends stopped answering Job 'because he was righteous in his own eyes' (32:1). Job has finished speaking. In many ways, there is nothing much left to say. But at this point a new voice is heard, that of Elihu, and he sets a rather different tone.

These chapters seem like another intrusion into the text. Indeed, many scholars regard them as secondary material added after the main portion of the drama was written. Their manner is different from what has gone before. Elihu does not feature in the initial conference on the ash heap. He does not get a mention with the other friends at the end of the drama in chapter 42. These chapters look like an interruption. But whatever the outcome of the schol-arly debate about their integrity within the book, they certainly serve in the edition in our Bibles as another breathing space between the final stand of Job in declaring his innocence, and the word of Yahweh spoken out of the whirlwind in chapter 38.

As we have already said, we need that breathing space. The artistic skill of the author of these chapters in sustaining the tension in Job, and also in preparing us carefully for the final word from the Lord, is unsurpassed. We need now to take stock of where the book of Job has led us – intellectually and spiritually. What have we learned from the debate? What do we yet need to hear?

The enigma of Elihu

Elihu is rather an enigma. He blusters on to the stage as an angry young man, full of his own importance, offering to clarify the situation for Job and his friends, angry with the muddle they have got themselves into. In one respect it is rather like a comic turn, for he manages to spend a lot of time not saying very much. He covers much of the ground of the other friends while supposedly saying something new. He claims to say more than the three friends have already said, and this is certainly true at the beginning and end of his speeches. But the middle speeches are cold and disappointing – a lapse into moralism which seems very hard on Job. Perhaps in these middle speeches Elihu is setting himself up as a sort of arbiter between Job and God. Perhaps he sees himself in a courtroom trying to argue out a case as coolly and dispassionately as he can. He is trying to set out the arguments for and against from the perspective of a detached observer. But the book of Job will not allow us to remain detached. We are inevitably caught up into its drama. That is perhaps why these middle speeches of Elihu do not take us much further at all, and leave us disappointed and frustrated. But as we shall see, at the start (chapter 32) and at the end (chapter 37), Elihu has something more constructive to offer.

A theological bridge?

The question still remains, however, as to why it is important to the author to have the Elihu speeches here at all. We have heard Job's passionate last stand. We are waiting for the Lord. How does Elihu serve to bring us from one to the other? Like chapter 28, Elihu opens up the theme of wisdom, which is a theological bridge in the story between Job's experience and his hearing the Lord. This will prove to be the theological significance of Elihu. But there is perhaps a dramatic purpose as well. These chapters give us a space between Job and Yahweh. They illustrate, just by being there, that Yahweh is not forced into a quick reply by the intensity of Job's entreaties. God acts in his own time, he is not at human beck and call. He 'comes down his own secret stair', and in sovereign and gracious care, he decides the timing of his interventions. Elihu gives us this place to pause, and so serves the author's purpose of displaying the freedom of God. Elihu blusters away, he makes his own mistakes. But in the middle of his blusterings, there are some gems, and it is these gems which are part of the preparation Job needs – and we the readers need – to be ready to hear the Lord.

a. Elihu's first speech (Job 32 – 33)
(See pp. 179–182.)

There are four speeches of Elihu's, the first of which begins at 32:6, following a short passage of prose which includes the reason for Elihu's anger:

> But Elihu son of Barakel the Buzite, of the family of Ram, became very angry with Job for justifying himself rather than God. ³He was also angry with the three friends, because they had found no way to refute Job, and yet had condemned him.

(32:2–3)

Elihu has waited until now to speak, in deference to the others' seniority (32:4), but their inability to offer much consolation to Job has also contributed to Elihu's anger (32:5).

He states his reasons for intervening in 32:6–22. He claims to have inspiration from God: 'But it is the spirit in a man, the breath of the Almighty, that gives him understanding' (32:8).

He has been reasoning with himself whether or not to intervene (32:16); but he cannot contain his anger any longer; he is ready to burst: 'inside I am like bottled-up wine, like new wineskins ready to burst' (32:19).

Elihu sounds pompous to us (32:10–12), though he may have seemed less so in the culture of the day, in which deference to age was so important. But the opening of chapter 33 seems patronizing and self-important on any account:

> But now, Job, listen to my words;
>   pay attention to everything I say.
> ²I am about to open my mouth;
>   my words are on the tip of my tongue.
> ³My words come from an upright heart;
>   my lips sincerely speak what I know.
> ⁴The Spirit of God has made me;
>   the breath of the Almighty gives me life.
> ⁵Answer me then, if you can;
>   prepare yourself and confront me.
> ⁶I am just like you before God;
>   I too have been taken from clay.
> ⁷No fear of me should alarm you,
>   nor should my hand be heavy upon you.

(33:1–7)

Elihu's main speech starts in 33:8. He quotes some of Job's complaints, and tries to answer them.

Elihu's case against Job

In the first place, says Elihu, Job has been complaining that God has simply ignored his sufferings by refusing to answer his prayer (33:13). In 33:14–18 Elihu replies in effect: Job, you are not right to claim that God has been ignoring you. 'God does speak' (33:14) – sometimes in dreams or visions. In fact God makes himself known in many different ways. Even in your nightmares, Job, God has been speaking to you: 'In a dream, in a vision of the night, when deep sleep falls on men as they slumber in their beds, he may speak in their ears and terrify them with warnings' (33:15–16).

God's purpose is to turn people aside from the way they are walking, to learn something more of the ways of God: 'to turn man from wrongdoing and keep him from pride, to preserve his soul from the pit, his life from perishing by the sword' (33:17–18).

Elihu is pointing to God's presence with Job even though Job has not been aware of it.

The second of Job's complaints, according to Elihu, is that God has been using his power unjustly. 'You have said . . . ". . . Go' has found fault with me . . . He fastens my feet in shackles; h keeps close watch on all my paths" ' (33:8–11).

This is answered by Elihu in 33:19–28. God may use even illnes and pain as a means of bringing chastening to the human spirit. 'A man may be chastened on a bed of pain, with constant distress in his bones' (33:19). God is not using his power in wanton fashion: sickness can act as a warning signal to make us sit up and take stock.

The third of Job's complaints to which Elihu draws attention is the claim that he is innocent. 'I am pure and without sin; I am clean and free from guilt' (33:9). Elihu comments that if a man accepts the chastening of sickness and prays to God, then God gives joy and salvation and a song. 'He prays to God and finds favour with him, he sees God's face and shouts for joy; he is restored by God to his righteous state' (33:26).

Elihu argues that God knows best

The summary of Elihu's first speech, therefore, is given in 33:12: 'You are not right; for God is greater than man.'

Elihu argues that God knows best – so what right has Job to complain? But there is more to it than this. One of the gems comes in 33:30, where Elihu tells us of God's purpose in suffering – it is both preventive and affirmative: 'to turn back his soul from the pit, that the light of life may shine on him.'

God allows his child to suffer 'to bring back his soul from the Pit' (RSV) – that is, to check him when he is on the wrong path; and 'that he may see the light of life' (RSV) – to bring him back on to the right path. In contrast to Eliphaz, Bildad and Zophar, therefore, Elihu has a more positive view of suffering. He is not seeing the situation in terms of past sins and Job's need for repentance; he is open to the possibility that God is doing some positive work in Job, even though Job could not see it. God is using Job's suffering creatively.

Creative suffering

It is very difficult to get this right. Express it one way and it sounds as though God is inflicting pain on his children for their good. That is surely misleading. There is no glorification of suffering here, even though some Christian people have sometimes been tempted down that path. Their mistake is that of the three friends, who found a causal link between sin and suffering, or between suffering and the good that can come from it.

In Luke 13, Jesus refers to the Galileans who had suffered death under Pilate, and to eighteen people who had died when the tower of Siloam fell on them.[3] 'Do you think,' he is asking, 'that these people were worse sinners than others because these disasters befell them? I tell you, No!' However, incidents like these call all of us to repentance. Jesus is clearly rejecting a causal link between sin and suffering in these cases. He rejects that link when his disciples ask him about the man born blind: ' "Who sinned, this man or his parents, that he was born blind?" "Neither this man nor his parents sinned," said Jesus, "but this happened so that the work of God might be displayed in his life." '[4]

Some Christians still fall into the trap of trying to link specific suffering with specific sins.

Elihu is somewhat clearer than this. The Swiss doctor Paul Tournier is clearer still. In his book *Creative Suffering*, Tournier quotes a remark of a Doctor Haynal as part of his discussion of the creative power of suffering:

What then of the relationship that exists between deprivation and suffering and creativity . . . ? But relationship is not the same as cause. You remember Dr Haynal's remark which I quoted: 'There is a relationship between the process of bereavement, loss,

---

[3] Lk. 13:1–5.   [4] Jn. 9:2–3.

deprivation and creativity.' He carefully refrains from saying that it is a relationship of cause and effect. The person matures, develops, becomes more creative, not because of the deprivation in itself, but through his own active response to misfortune, through the struggle to come to terms with it, and morally to overcome it, even if in spite of everything there is no cure . . . That is the trap, to confuse relationship with cause, and hence to say that suffering is good for one. The distinction is a subtle one, but it is vital.[5]

A further point is made by Simone Weil in her meditations on the Christian faith, and the vocation of suffering to which Christ calls some people: 'The extreme greatness of Christianity lies in the fact that it does not seek a supernatural remedy for suffering, but a supernatural use for it.'[6]

In his own way, Elihu is beginning to grope towards this truth. He is starting to show Job that through his struggle to come to terms with his misfortune, God is at work.

b. Elihu's second speech (Job 34)
(See pp. 182–184.)

By contrast with what has just gone before, Elihu's second speech is very disappointing. In chapter 34, Elihu turns his attention away from Job and towards the 'wise men' (34:2). Does he mean just the three friends who (we are to assume) are now a little downstage, or is he also including other bystanders who might be listening to this conversation between Elihu and Job?

Elihu now sides with these 'wise men' in an attack on Job's piety:

> [2]*Hear my words, you wise men;*
> *listen to me, you men of learning.*
> [3]*For the ear tests words*
> *as the tongue tastes food.*
> [4]*Let us discern for ourselves what is right;*
> *let us learn together what is good.*
>
> [5]*Job says, 'I am innocent,*
> *but God denies me justice.*

[5] P. Tournier, *Creative Suffering* (Eng. tr., SCM Press, 1982), p. 28.
[6] S. Weil, *Gravity and Grace* (Routledge, Ark Paperbacks, 3rd ed., 1987).

> *⁶Although I am right,*
> *I am considered a liar;*
> *although I am guiltless,*
> *his arrow inflicts an incurable wound.'*
>
> (34:2–6)

This leads to an appalling insult: 'What man is like Job, who drinks scorn like water? He keeps company with evildoers; he associates with wicked men' (34:7–8).

Elihu defends God's justice

Now any pastoral insight which Elihu may have had in his first speech seems to have disappeared. Face to face with the 'wise men', Elihu seems to have become cold and detached. Perhaps he is the sort of person whose views change depending on whom he is talking to. He speaks to the wise men about God, trying to justify the ways of God to Job. 'It is unthinkable that God would do wrong, that the Almighty would pervert justice' (34:12). It is all so clinical. He begins with God's power (34:13–20), but it is clear that God, for Elihu in this speech, is merely the impersonal powerful administrator of justice (34:19). Elihu then talks about God's knowledge (34:21–23) and God's impartiality (34:24–27).

Elihu's God is a God of almighty justice. Is he the author of all things? Is he the author of evil? Elihu seems to get very near to saying so here. For him, might is right. There is no hint, of course, of that other story between God and the Satan, of which we were told at the beginning. We know that there is a difference here between God's perfect ordering of the world, and God's permissive will in which, for reasons of his own, he lets the Satan have some rein. All unknown to Job and to Elihu, God and the Satan are working some inscrutable providence in which Job's own fortunes are caught up. But Elihu presumes to understand! Yet his only way of understanding the ways of God is in terms of God's power and might. He says a lot about divine justice, but not a word about divine grace. The speech can be summarized by 34:11: 'He repays a man for what he has done; he brings upon him what his conduct deserves.' Here Elihu is rationalizing the orthodoxy of desert ('You get what you deserve'). We are back again to Eliphaz's faulty logic.

The chapter concludes with a discussion of Job's foolishness:

> *³¹Suppose a man says to God,*
> *'I am guilty but will offend no more.*
> *³²Teach me what I cannot see;*
> *if I have done wrong, I will not do so again.'*

127

> ³³*Should God then reward you on your terms,*
> *when you refuse to repent?*
> *You must decide, not I;*
> *so tell me what you know.*
>
> ³⁴*Men of understanding declare,*
> *wise men who hear me say to me,*
> ³⁵'*Job speaks without knowledge;*
> *his words lack insight.*'
> ³⁶*Oh, that Job might be tested to the utmost*
> *for answering like a wicked man!*
> ³⁷*To his sin he adds rebellion;*
> *scornfully he claps his hands among us*
> *and multiplies his words against God.*

(34:31–37)

c. Elihu's third speech (Job 35)
(See pp. 184–185.)

Elihu says God is distant and detached

In his third speech (chapter 35), Elihu begins to take up Job's complaints again. Job had asked, 'What is the use of being good?' (*cf.* 34:9). This is now unpacked into two further questions.

First, 'What do I gain by not sinning?' (35:3). This question is augmented by quotations from Job's earlier statements in chapters 7, 9 and 22 – referred to here in verses 5 to 7 – to which Elihu replies that nothing at all is gained by sinning or not sinning: You have only to look at the heavens and the clouds to realize that God is so much higher than us that none of our actions can affect him for good or ill. Nothing anyone does either hurts or helps God (35:8). Elihu is again falling back into the old argument we heard before from Eliphaz.

By taking this unhelpful tack, Elihu in fact boxes himself into a corner. As Francis Andersen puts it:

If he is saying that God's intrinsic righteousness is perfect, not capable of being augmented by human goodness, not capable of being diminished by human wickedness, then the idea is a very abstract one, and an evasion. If it means that God couldn't care less about human conduct either way, then he is echoing opinions quoted in verses 6 and 7 and has undermined his whole case, saying in effect that justice means nothing to God. Beginning with impartiality, he has ended with indifference.[7]

The second of Job's questions is in effect: 'Why doesn't God answer prayer?' Elihu's answer to this is equally thoughtless and heartless. He gives three quick reasons why prayer is not answered: pride (35:12); wrong motives (35:13); lack of faith (35:14). This is all very worthy at the theoretical level, but Elihu is holding on to his theory at the expense of missing Job's predicament. None of these reasons counts for Job, for what matters to him is that from a clean heart he has sought the Lord, but so far he has always seemed to receive the stern reply, 'No answer.'

So Elihu is proving to be something of a disappointment, even after a promising start. He may be, as we suggested, setting himself up as an adjudicator. Perhaps the writer presents him in this way as an illustration of the best that unaided human wisdom can offer. Here is the 'human perspective'. It does not take us very far. We really do need more than this, as Elihu's final speech will show.

'The wild order of things'

Elihu so far seems to have a God who is manageable and predictable, whom he can understand. God's ways are clear to him. Everything is under control. But if we have learned anything so far from the book of Job, it is that reality is much less clear, manageable and predictable than we would like to think. The divine wisdom, we are realizing, is not merely something that we can get if we think hard enough, or behave well enough, or if our theological system is coherent, tidy and clear. The divine wisdom, as we shall see, comes by way of the storm and the whirlwind. In a phrase from a poem by Professor Frances Young, 'wisdom' takes on another aspect. 'Wisdom' is the 'wild order of things'.

The poem is called 'Sophie's call' (echoing deliberately the Greek word for wisdom, sōphia). It is a long poem; this is just a part of it:

> In a night of loss comes Sophie's call.
> Visions in a dark night of passion and loss.
> She appears lovely in her element.
> I see her as the wild order of things.
> Her beauty is the strain of a mountain stream.
> Filling the conscious mind with unconscious tone
> Intoning the tones of grey-green clouds and rocks

[7] Andersen, p. 256.

Older than ever ancient sages dreamed.
Sophie's eyes are deep pools of love.
Aged with wisdom, yet dancing with glistening spray,
As catching the droplets of light, her youthful hair
Is tossed in the breeze. . . .

This wild beauty I see at the heart of things;
Conceived in the mind of the unknown Ancient of Days
She is the elemental principle,
The underlying pattern beneath the chaos. . . .

'I am Sophie, the wild order of things.' . . . [8]

There is a wildness to the divine ordering of things which the
Elihus of this world cannot stand. Elihu cannot bear very much
reality.

C. S. Lewis makes a similar point when Mr Beaver points out
that Aslan is not a tame lion:

> Mr. Beaver had warned them. 'He'll be coming and going,' he
> had said. 'One day you'll see him and another you won't. He
> doesn't like being tied down – and of course he has other coun-
> tries to attend to. It's quite all right. He'll often drop in. Only
> you mustn't press him. He's wild, you know. Not like a *tame*
> lion.'[9]

Elihu's God is too tidy and too small.

Songs in the night

There is, though, a further gem in this third speech of Elihu which
we must not miss. It is a phrase of beauty and comfort. Job 35:10
describes God as one 'who gives songs in the night'. In the darkness, Elihu knows it is possible to sing the song of the Creator.
Elihu himself so far seems a long way from showing Job how.
But that is a phrase of great comfort for people searching for
a hand in the darkness. The Creator God is one who 'gives
songs in the night'. May he give us grace so to know him in the
darknesses we face that we may with joy be enabled to sing his
songs.

[8] From 'Sophie's Call', an unpublished poem by Frances Young, quoted with the
author's permission.
[9] C. S. Lewis, *The Lion, the Witch and the Wardrobe* (Fontana ed., 1980),
p. 165.

d. Elihu's final speech (Job 36 – 37)
(See pp. 185–188.)

Chapters 36 to 37 are Elihu's final speech. Now, thank goodness, things have changed again for the better. Towards the wise men in chapter 34, Elihu has come over as the victim of his own cold rationalism, and as one who colludes with others in the criticism of their erstwhile friend. Towards Job in chapter 35, he has been callous and insensitive. But now in chapters 36 to 37 Elihu is turned towards God, and the tone is softer; the pastoral sensitivity returns, and we are given not only the best statement so far of the theology of rewards and punishments, but important new insights as well. There are some more gems here.

In the book of Job, these chapters form a bridge between the world of Eliphaz, Bildad and Zophar, and the word of the Lord from the whirlwind. They soften us, prepare us, and begin to show us what an encounter with the Lord will be like.

> ⁵*God is mighty, but does not despise men;*
> *he is mighty, and firm in his purpose.*
> ⁶*He does not keep the wicked alive*
> *but gives the afflicted their rights.*
> ⁷*He does not take his eyes off the righteous;*
> *he enthrones them with kings*
> *and exalts them for ever.*
> ⁸*But if men are bound in chains,*
> *held fast by cords of affliction,*
> ⁹*he tells them what they have done –*
> *that they have sinned arrogantly.*
> ¹⁰*He makes them listen to correction*
> *and commands them to repent of their evil.*
> ¹¹*If they obey and serve him,*
> *they will spend the rest of their days in prosperity*
> *and their years in contentment.*
> ¹²*But if they do not listen,*
> *they will perish by the sword*
> *and die without knowledge.*
>
> (36:5–12)

Elihu begins by repeating the thought that though God sends trouble, he is just and merciful (36:6). God protectively watches over the righteous (36:7). Elihu recognizes at last the pain of being caught in the 'cords of affliction' (36:8). He outlines the conventional wisdom: 'If they obey and serve him: prosperity; if they do not listen: they perish and die' (*cf.* 36:11–12).

The pain that heals

Then comes a new insight: then comes the most profound thing which Elihu ever says. Speaking of God, he says, 'Those who suffer he delivers in their suffering; he speaks to them in their affliction' (36:15).

This is not simply saying again that God uses suffering to chasten and to bring to repentance. It is saying much more. Elihu is here recognizing that through the very process of affliction, there can be deliverance. There can be, in the title of Martin Israel's book, 'the pain that heals'.[10] It is through the suffering of God's servant that there can be healing.

We may recall how Eustace in *The Voyage of the 'Dawn Treader'* was trying to get rid of the dragon skin in which he had been trapped, and scraped away one set of scales only to find another underneath:

> 'Then the lion said – but I don't know if it spoke – You will have to let me undress you. I was afraid of his claws, I can tell you, but I was pretty near desperate now. . . . The very first tear he made was so deep that I thought it had gone right into my heart. And when he began pulling the skin off, it hurt worse than anything I've ever felt. . . . Then he caught hold of me – I didn't like that much for I was very tender underneath now that I'd no skin on – and threw me into the water. It smarted like anything but only for a moment. After that it became perfectly delicious and as soon as I started swimming and splashing I found that all the pain had gone from my arm. And then I saw why. I had turned into a boy again.'[11]

That is Elihu's point. God's dealings with us, though painful, says Elihu, are for healing. God is compassionate, luring us back into his ways, opening our eyes to a new world, opening our ears to new voices and new songs. He is pointing to a theme picked up by Martin Israel when he says: 'It is one of the fundamental contributions of pain to make people wake up to a deeper quality of existence and to seek evidence for meaning in their lives beyond the immediate sensations that arrest their attention.'[12]

[10] M. Israel, *The Pain that Heals* (Hodder & Stoughton, 1981).
[11] C. S. Lewis, *The Voyage of the Dawn Treader* (Penguin Books ed., 1965), p. 96.   [12] Israel, *The Pain that Heals*, p. 12.

God's power in the storm

To prepare us for the coming of the Lord, the dramatist now gives Elihu a marvellous speech extolling the greatness of God (36:22 – 37:24), opening our hearts to ever deeper levels of understanding. Even innocent Job can learn more of the deep things of God.

Elihu moves us from a word about the divine power (36:22) to a wonderful picture of God in the storm. The last few verses of chapter 36 describe the rainstorm:

> ²⁷*He draws up the drops of water,*
> *which distil as rain to the streams;*
> ²⁸*the clouds pour down their moisture*
> *and abundant showers fall on mankind.*
> ²⁹*Who can understand how he spreads out the clouds,*
> *how he thunders from his pavilion?*
> ³⁰*See how he scatters his lightning about him,*
> *bathing the depths of the sea.*
> ³¹*This is the way he governs the nations*
> *and provides food in abundance.*
> ³²*He fills his hands with lightning*
> *and commands it to strike its mark .*
> ³³*His thunder announces the coming storm;*
> *even the cattle make known its approach.*
>
> (36:27–33)

It leads on into chapter 37 with a description of the lightning and thunder. 'God thunders wondrously with his voice; he does great things which we cannot comprehend' (*cf.* 37:5). Then the cold chill of winter covers everything:

> ⁶*He says to the snow, 'Fall on the earth,'*
> *and to the rain shower, 'Be a mighty downpour.'*
> ⁷*So that all men he has made may know his work,*
> *he stops every man from his labour.*
> ⁸*The animals take cover;*
> *they remain in their dens.*
> ⁹*The tempest comes out from its chamber,*
> *the cold from the driving winds.*
> ¹⁰*The breath of God produces ice,*
> *and the broad waters become frozen.*
> ¹¹*He loads the clouds with moisture;*
> *he scatters his lightning through them.*

> ¹²*At his direction they swirl around*
> *over the face of the whole earth*
> *to do whatever he commands them.*
> ¹³*He brings the clouds to punish men,*
> *or to water his earth and show his love.*

(37:6–13)

This is a picture of a world in which harsh things happen. By the breath of God, ice is given. It is a picture of the world in which Job is struggling. He has felt the force of the storm; he has heard the crashing of the thunder. He has been frozen by God's ice.

But it is for God's purposes – even of love – that God causes this to happen. The storm both disciplines and refreshes the land. Both discipline and refreshment are expressions of his faithful, steadfast love. 'He brings the clouds to punish men, or to water his earth and show his love' (37:13).

Then things begin to ease up just a little. From verse 21, the storm is over; the skies clear; the light brightens, and all becomes tranquil again. 'Out of the north he comes in golden splendour: God comes in awesome majesty' (37:22).

> ²¹*Now no-one can look at the sun,*
> *bright as it is in the skies*
> *after the wind has swept them clean.*
> ²²*Out of the north he comes in golden splendour;*
> *God comes in awesome majesty.*
> ²³*The Almighty is beyond our reach and exalted in power;*
> *in his justice and great righteousness he does not oppress.*
> ²⁴*Therefore, men revere him,*
> *for does he not have regard for all the wise in heart?'*

(37:21–24)

We must take care to notice what has happened in this speech. Elihu has now pointed us up to God. The book of Job is now ready for the sun to rise again on Job and bring him some peace in the morning of springtime.

3. Transforming the question

Both Job and his friends have been looking for an answer, looking for a cause. But all the searching for causes has proved useless. The three friends have ultimately had no answer for Job. The answer comes not in looking back, but in looking up. We must look forwards for the divine purpose, not hunt around for causes in the past. Elihu has moved us from a backward-looking, retributive understanding of suffering to a forward-looking, redemptive one. There is a pain which heals.

Jesus said the same, we recall, to his disciples when they asked about the man who was born blind. 'Neither this man nor his parents sinned, but this happened so that the work of God might be displayed in his life'.[13] The question 'Why?' is transformed into the question 'For what purpose?', and the answer is not in the sins of the past, but in the manifestation of the works of God in the future.

This is the point to which Elihu has brought us.

Beginning with the traditional orthodoxy of the scribal schools, the law of retribution and reward, the narrow wisdom of the three friends, Elihu has moved us on. He has taken us from an exploration of God's power, and a meditation on the greatness of God, through the storm, to his conclusion in 37:24. The NIV reads: 'Therefore, men revere him, for does he not have regard for all the wise in heart?' Andersen's translation may be better:

Therefore men fear Him,
Surely all wise men of heart fear him.[14]

The fear of the Lord, that is where we have come to – and the fear of the Lord, as we learned earlier in chapter 28, is the beginning of wisdom.

A glimpse of wisdom

Elihu is thus a bridge in the book of Job, stretching from the inadequate theology of a detached God – a God of power, might, majesty and dominion but detached from human pain and experience – to the need for Wisdom. We are enabled to glimpse the divine Wisdom, the 'wild order of things', and to receive his gift to enable us to cope. We are brought to the 'fear of the Lord', the way of living before God in obedience and dependence on grace: that experience of the Lord's active presence which Wisdom implies.

Eliphaz had such a transcendent God that he was totally unconcerned with the trivia of Job's life. Elihu now tells us of the fear of the Lord, that intimate relationship in which the Lord is very much concerned with the small as well as the big aspects of our very human experience.

Elihu has brought us from theology to wisdom, from argument

[13] Jn. 9:3.   [14] Andersen, p. 268.

135

and despair to God himself. So he has brought us in his way to where the Hymn to Wisdom in Job 28 also brought us. We need to meet the Lord in grace; we need to begin with the fear of the Lord, in communion with him.

This idea that wisdom is not the accumulation of knowledge, be it technical or theological, but a way of living before God, comes to its sharpest focus in Paul's teaching that Christ is 'the power of God and the wisdom of God'.[15] Wisdom is Christ in his vulnerability, his self-giving, and his suffering. Wisdom is Christ in his obedience to the Father even to death on the cross.

In Jesus the divine Wisdom is displayed, and by the grace of the Spirit is made available to us. It is the wisdom of the suffering servant of the Lord, by whose sufferings fellowship with the Lord is found.

That is the path of pilgrimage which Job himself is treading. He is learning the hard way to Wisdom: 'the wild order of things'. He has been learning to cope.

He is unwittingly providing his own answer to the Satan's question: 'Does Job serve God for naught?' There is no reward other than fellowship with God himself, which is the gift of his grace. That is where our final chapter will take us.

[15] 1 Cor. 1:24.

5. The Lord speaks
(Job 38 – 42)

At long last, the Lord speaks: 'Then the LORD answered Job out of the storm' (38:1).

It is a long while since we were in the heavenly court, hearing the Satan taunt God with his question, 'Does Job fear God for nothing?' We saw God give the Satan some rein in testing Job's integrity by taking away everything that he had. The Satan does not feature directly in the story any more. As Karl Barth put it, a short sharp look at him sufficed! It is a long time since Job's wife tempted him to curse God and die, and since his friends sat with him for seven days and seven nights in the compassion of their silent presence.

Since then we have heard the three cycles of speeches, with the friends offering their rationalized version of the orthodoxy of retribution and desert. They assumed Job must have sinned, and they called on him to repent. We heard them extolling God's majesty and power, but saying little about his loving presence and grace. The poet has pointed us to the fear of the Lord which is the beginning of wisdom, and Elihu's theological reflections eventually pointed there also.

Throughout, Job has asserted his innocence and integrity. He has wept and raged, been in despair and anguish of soul. His body, mind and spirit have all been troubled. He has constantly struggled with this tension in the very fibres of his being: he is being treated unjustly, and yet there must be justice in this world! Again and again he calls on God to make himself known. Why is God so unfair, so distant, so silent?

Now God speaks from 'the whirlwind' (38:1, RSV).There have been hints of this and preparations for it: the Elihu interlude took us through the storm to the calm at the other side, and Job himself has held on to the hope of an umpire, a vindicator, a redeemer. It may not happen in this world, but God will surely answer him one day!

God answers Job

Chapter 38 tells us that God does answer Job. He does so in this world, in sovereign freedom, and in God's timing. The Elihu speeches, which came after Job's last stand, prevent us from thinking that God is somehow forced into a reply by Job's persistence in his previous speech. Throughout these last few chapters, though, the drums have been rolling, and the climax of the book is now upon us.

At first sight, it is a big disappointment. In chapters 38 and 39, the writer takes us on a tour of the heavens, the sea, the stars and various animals, and then he tells us to look at Behemoth, the hippopotamus (40:15), and Leviathan, the crocodile (41:1). It is all rather surprising.

As the Archdeacon muses in Charles Williams' novel *War in Heaven*: 'As a mere argument, there's something lacking perhaps, in saying to a man who's lost his money and his house and his family and is sitting on the dustbin, all over boils, "Look at the hippopotamus." '[1]

God gives no answer to Job's questions, no apology for having been silent for so long, no hint about Satan's wager, no apparent acknowledgment of Job's struggle. Is it really enough?

This has led many commentators to presume that, despite the magnificent poetry of these chapters (especially chapters 38 and 39, which must rank among the finest nature poetry of the world), they are additions to the text of Job and must be discounted.

But before we succumb to so radical a view, let us take time to ask a little more closely what is going on.

There are five main points to draw from these chapters, and then there is an epilogue.

1. Yahweh speaks

The first and most significant thing is that God speaks! God makes himself known. Elsewhere in the Bible, the storm is the appropriate context for a theophany – that is, a disclosure of God's presence. In the epoch-making disclosure of God to Moses on Mount Sinai, God came to the mountain in the storm:

On the morning of the third day there was thunder and lightning,

[1] C. Williams, *War in Heaven* (Faber ed., 1947), p. 24.

with thick cloud over the mountain, and a very loud trumpet blast. . . . Then Moses led the people out of the camp to meet with God, and they stood at the foot of the mountain. Mount Sinai was covered with smoke, because the LORD descended on it in fire. The smoke billowed up from it like smoke from a furnace, the whole mountain trembled violently, and the sound of the trumpet grew louder and louder. Then Moses spoke and the voice of God answered him.[2]

The thunderstorm with its lightning, cloud and noise both disclosed and hid the majesty of God. God came to speak to the people hidden in a dense cloud.[3] Cloud was a frequent symbol of God's presence. On Mount Sinai, God came to his people in the full garments of his terrifying holiness. The theme is similar in the book of Job. God does not condescend to come down (as he comes down to see what is going on at the Tower of Babel in Genesis 11). He makes himself known as *mysterium tremendum et fascinans*,[4] an inviting yet terrifying mystery.

The prophet Nahum also tells us that 'His way is in the whirlwind and the storm'.[5] That is a text we do well to keep in mind whenever we are tempted by the sloppiest sort of devotional literature to believe that the life of faith is really a bed of roses. Alongside all we rightly want to say about Christian joy and the gift of peace which garrisons our hearts and minds in Christ Jesus,[6] we also know and must affirm that 'his way is in the whirlwind and storm'. It is from the whirlwind that God speaks to Job.

'Yahweh'

And the one who speaks is 'Yahweh', the covenant Lord. God had been given his personal covenant name, Yahweh, in the prologue to the book of Job. There we were introduced to Job, and were invited to reflect on God's personal relationship with him. Throughout chapters 3 to 37, the name Yahweh is not used; God is called *El Shaddai*, God the Almighty. In the book of Job this has become a way of speaking of God as detached and distant. The basic revelation of God as 'Shaddai' was given in Genesis, and there it was the picture of a God who took over when all hope was gone and all strength exhausted. It was to the care of 'Shaddai', for example, that Jacob committed Benjamin when the brothers asked to take him back with them to Egypt.[7] It was 'Shaddai' who took

---

[2] Ex. 19:16–19.   [3] Ex. 19:9.
[4] Rudolf Otto, *The Idea of the Holy* (1917; Eng. tr., Oxford University Press, 1923).
[5] Na. 1:3.   [6] Phil. 4:7.   [7] Gn. 43:14.

139

care of Joseph.[8] But with Eliphaz, Bildad and Zophar, 'Shaddai' has become a God not of personal grace and security, but of distance, detachment and impersonal almighty power. They had got used to using a name of God which originally spoke of grace in a way that denied grace. How barren theology can become when it loses touch with the gracious heart of God! The personal closeness of the covenant Lord has given way to the distance of God's majesty and might.

But now, in chapter 38 our author wants us to be in no doubt. God is called 'Yahweh' once again. Now the gracious Lord of the covenant promise to Abraham is speaking to this man from Uz. Now the God whose name 'Yahweh' is associated with his personal presence of care, steadfast love and faithfulness to the people of his covenant, *this* God speaks to Job.

The Lord does come!

We recall the depths of Job's cry in chapter 23:

> If only I knew where to find him,
>   if only I could go to his dwelling!
> But if I go to the east, he is not there;
>   if I go to the west, I do not find him.
> When he is at work in the north, I do not see him;
>   when he turns to the south, I catch no glimpse of him.
>   (23:3, 8–9)

Job's worst fears were that God had abandoned him. In the silence and the isolation, he had assumed that God had let him down and let him go. Job did not know that God had taken a risk, so to speak, to demonstrate Job's integrity for heavenly purposes of his own. Of course God's withdrawal was all part of the story, for Job's pilgrimage of faith was precisely *not* a pilgrimage of sight. It is crucial to the story that Job should be in the dark. So he stands as a representative of, and an example for, all those of us who try to keep trusting in the dark. For all those of us whose faith is tested by the darkness and the apparent absence of God, the great reassurance of Job 38 is that God speaks. The Lord does come!

God has, in truth, been present all along. Now that presence is made known. This is the first and greatest reassurance for Job. The Lord comes. God makes himself known. That is the most important thing these chapters have to say.

[8] Gn. 49:25.

140

The well-known anonymous meditation 'Footprints' expresses this well:

> One night a man had a dream. He dreamed he was walking along the beach with the Lord. Across the sky flashed scenes from his life. For each scene, he noticed two sets of footprints in the sand: one belonging to him, and the other to the Lord.
>
> When the last scene of his life flashed before him, he looked back at the footprints in the sand. He noticed that many times along the path of his life there was only one set of footprints. He also noticed that it happened at the very lowest and saddest times in his life.
>
> This really bothered him and he questioned the Lord about it. 'Lord, you said that once I decided to follow you, you'd walk with me all the way. But I have noticed that during the most troublesome times in my life, there is only one set of footprints. I don't understand why when I needed you most you would leave me.'
>
> The Lord replied, 'My son, my precious child, I love you and I would never leave you. During your times of trial and suffering, when you see only one set of footprints, it was then that I carried you.'

Or, as Oswald Chambers put it: 'A man up against things feels that he has lost God, while in reality, he has come face to face with Him.'[9]

2. The wisdom of God is seen in his creation (Job 38 – 39)

This is the moment for us to allow these wonderful texts to speak for themselves:

> *Then the* LORD *answered Job out of the storm. He said:*
>
> [2]*'Who is this that darkens my counsel*
> *with words without knowledge?*
> [3]*Brace yourself like a man;*
> *I will question you,*
> *and you shall answer me.*
>
> [4]*'Where were you when I laid the earth's foundation?*
> *Tell me, if you understand.*
> [5]*Who marked off its dimensions? Surely you know!*

---

[9] Chambers, p. 18.

141

Who stretched a measuring line across it?
⁶On what were its footings set,
  or who laid its cornerstone –
⁷while the morning stars sang together
  and all the angels shouted for joy?

⁸'Who shut up the sea behind doors
  when it burst forth from the womb,
⁹when I made the clouds its garment
  and wrapped it in thick darkness,
¹⁰when I fixed limits for it
  and set its doors and bars in place,
¹¹when I said, "This far you may come and no farther,
  here is where your proud waves halt"?

¹²'Have you ever given orders to the morning,
  or shown the dawn its place,
¹³that it might take the earth by the edges
  and shake the wicked out of it?
¹⁴The earth takes shape like clay under a seal;
  its features stand out like those of a garment.
¹⁵The wicked are denied their light,
  and their upraised arm is broken.

¹⁶'Have you journeyed to the springs of the sea
  or walked in the recesses of the deep?
¹⁷Have the gates of death been shown to you?
  Have you seen the gates of the shadow of death?
¹⁸Have you comprehended the vast expanses of the earth?
  Tell me, if you know all this.

¹⁹'What is the way to the abode of light?
  And where does darkness reside?
²⁰Can you take them to their places?
  Do you know the paths to their dwellings?
²¹Surely you know, for you were already born!
  You have lived so many years!

²²'Have you entered the storehouses of the snow
  or seen the storehouses of the hail,
²³which I reserve for times of trouble,
  for days of war and battle?
²⁴What is the way to the place where the lightning is
  dispersed,

*or the place where the east winds are scattered over the
   earth?*
²⁵*Who cuts a channel for the torrents of rain,
   and a path for the thunderstorm,*
²⁶*to water a land where no man lives,
   a desert with no-one in it,*
²⁷*to satisfy a desolate wasteland
   and make it sprout with grass?*
²⁸*Does the rain have a father?
   Who fathers the drops of dew?*
²⁹*From whose womb comes the ice?
   Who gives birth to the frost from the heavens*
³⁰*when the waters become hard as stone,
   when the surface of the deep is frozen?*

³¹*'Can you bind the beautiful Pleiades?
   Can you loose the cords of Orion?*
³²*Can you bring forth the constellations in their seasons
   or lead out the Bear with its cubs?*
³³*Do you know the laws of the heavens?
   Can you set up God's dominion over the earth?*

³⁴*'Can you raise your voice to the clouds
   and cover yourself with a flood of water?*
³⁵*Do you send the lightning bolts on their way?
   Do they report to you, "Here we are"?*
³⁶*Who endowed the heart with wisdom
   or gave understanding to the mind?*
³⁷*Who has the wisdom to count the clouds?
   Who can tip over the water jars of the heavens*
³⁸*when the dust becomes hard
   and the clods of earth stick together?*

³⁹*'Do you hunt the prey for the lioness
   and satisfy the hunger of the lions*
⁴⁰*when they crouch in their dens
   or lie in wait in a thicket?*
⁴¹*Who provides food for the raven
   when its young cry out to God
   and wander about for lack of food?*

^{39:1}*'Do you know when the mountain goats give birth?
   Do you watch when the doe bears her fawn?*
²*Do you count the months till they bear?*

Do you know the time they give birth?
³*They crouch down and bring forth their young;*
their labour pains are ended.
⁴*Their young thrive and grow strong in the wilds;*
they leave and do not return.

⁵*'Who let the wild donkey go free?*
Who untied his ropes?
⁶*I gave him the wasteland as his home,*
the salt flats as his habitat.
⁷*He laughs at the commotion in the town;*
he does not hear a driver's shout.
⁸*He ranges the hills for his pasture*
and searches for any green thing.

⁹*'Will the wild ox consent to serve you?*
Will he stay by your manger at night?
¹⁰*Can you hold him to the furrow with a harness?*
Will he till the valleys behind you?
¹¹*Will you rely on him for his great strength?*
Will you leave your heavy work to him?
¹²*Can you trust him to bring in your grain*
and gather it to your threshing-floor?

¹³*'The wings of the ostrich flap joyfully,*
but they cannot compare with the pinions and feathers
of the stork.
¹⁴*She lays her eggs on the ground*
and lets them warm in the sand,
¹⁵*unmindful that a foot may crush them,*
that some wild animal may trample them.
¹⁶*She treats her young harshly, as if they were not hers;*
she cares not that her labour was in vain,
¹⁷*for God did not endow her with wisdom*
or give her a share of good sense.
¹⁸*Yet when she spreads her feathers to run,*
she laughs at horse and rider.

¹⁹*'Do you give the horse his strength*
or clothe his neck with a flowing mane?
²⁰*Do you make him leap like a locust,*
striking terror with his proud snorting?
²¹*He paws fiercely, rejoicing in his strength,*
and charges into the fray.

²²*He laughs at fear, afraid of nothing;*
he does not shy away from the sword.
²³*The quiver rattles against his side,*
along with the flashing spear and lance.
²⁴*In frenzied excitement he eats up the ground;*
he cannot stand still when the trumpet sounds.
²⁵*At the blast of the trumpet he snorts, "Aha!"*
He catches the scent of battle from afar,
the shout of commanders and the battle cry.

²⁶*'Does the hawk take flight by your wisdom*
and spread his wings towards the south?
²⁷*Does the eagle soar at your command*
and build his nest on high?
²⁸*He dwells on a cliff and stays there at night;*
a rocky crag is his stronghold.
²⁹*From there he seeks out his food;*
his eyes detect it from afar.
³⁰*His young ones feast on blood,*
and where the slain are, there is he.'

Why, we need to ask, does God spend all this time talking about the skies and the stars and the animals? Surely there is a more appropriate topic of conversation for someone who for some weeks has been going through an appalling sense of isolation?

It is, of course, only when a depressed person has the safety and reassurance of another's presence that conversation can happen. Now that Job knows he is not alone, it is appropriate for God to talk – and perhaps to distract Job from his misery, certainly to give him new perspectives on his situation.

We need to try to catch the tone of this to grasp its meaning. God is going to question Job: 'Brace yourself like a man; I will question you, and you shall answer me' (38:3). It sounds rather threatening, and some commentators take this to mean that God is going to overpower and humiliate Job, by showing him his foolishness and his impertinence. However, it may rather be that there is a gentle irony to the tone, and the questions are not threatening, but rather educative: the sort of questions a good teacher may ask a child in order to elicit understanding. It is as though the Lord God is taking a walk through his creation – a walk through the Garden, perhaps, as the storm becomes still – and is inviting Job to accompany him: Do you see this . . . ? Do you recognize that . . . ? As Jesus later invited his disciples to 'consider the lilies',[10] so here God is inviting Job to consider the beauty and order and wonder of the created world.

The skies

Let me amaze you, says God, by the complexity and intricacy of it all! From the foundation of the earth (38:4), when the morning stars sang together and all the sons of God in the heavenly court shouted for joy (38:7), that joyous celebration of the Creator has been sung ever since. Consider the sea, held back from its chaotic power (38:8–11), the skies, the deep, the light, and the darkness (38:12–21). Have you entered the storehouses of the snow, or of the hail (38:22)? And what about the rain (38:25–30)? Then lift your eyes to the heavens, to the Pleiades and Orion, to the clouds, the lightning and the mists (28:31–38). Do you see these things? Come round with me and enjoy my creation: marvel at its wonders: see how it all fits together into an overriding pattern and purpose.

The animals

Think of the animals too! Can you hunt prey for the lioness (38:39)? Who provides for the ravens (38:41)? What about the life-giving power of birth – for the mountain goats (39:1); the wild asses (39:5); the wild oxen (39:9)?

Then comes one of God's jokes – the ostrich (39:13)! The silly bird, flapping her wings proudly but getting nowhere, leaving her eggs in the earth not thinking that someone may step on them (39:15). God did not give her a share of good sense (39:17)! Even those parts of God's creation which seem deficient in wisdom are still part of the divine wild ordering of things. Indeed, the ostrich is almost a picture of Job himself – a paradox, a mixture of strength (39:18) and foolishness (39:13–17). Yet in spite of all its failure to understand, it has a valued place in God's creation. And what about the war-horse? In a magnificent passage of descriptive poetry (39:19–25), we can hear him tossing back his proud mane, snorting and pawing the ground, thundering into battle as the trumpet sounds. The soaring hawk, the mighty eagle (39:26–27): these, too, are part of the world created by the divine wisdom.

Come round with me, Job: see these things; wonder at them; enjoy them. You cannot control them, but they are under my control, says God.

By an act of understanding, therefore, be present now with all the creatures among which you live; and hear them in their

---

[10] Mt. 6:28, RSV.

beings and operations praising God in an heavenly manner. Some of them vocally, others in their ministry, all of them naturally and continually. We infinitely wrong ourselves by laziness and confinement. All creatures in all nations and tongues and people praise God infinitely; and the more for being your whole and perfect treasures. You are never what you ought till you go out of yourself and walk among them.[11]

'You are never what you ought, till you go out of yourself and walk among them.' That is perhaps why God takes Job on this tour – to show his majesty in his works: to take Job out of himself, to distract him from his misery, to broaden his horizons to the creative and life-giving majesty of God, and especially to enable him to see himself in a new setting.

Job, this is where your heart will find rest: in finding your own place within the panorama of God's purposes for his world.Can you lift your eyes from the ash heap, and see the glory of God in his creation? Then you may glimpse again how, as Traherne puts it elsewhere, to 'enjoy the world'.

Enjoy the world

There is a simple, but not unimportant, pastoral application to be made here. God, we are told in Genesis, made the man and put him in a garden that was 'pleasant to the sight'.[12] The context in which we live our lives contributes significantly to our sense of well-being. The ash heap may be an appropriate place on which to sit if we are in mourning, but it is no place to stay if we wish to feel better. Sometimes we will most help distressed people – help them draw nearer to God, from the depths of depression – not by teaching them doctrine, or by preaching our best sermon, or by showing them the error of their ways, but by walking with them round the garden, by taking them to see a waterfall or a sunset, by helping them recover an enjoyment in the world. Such steps are not always practicable, of course. But in so far as we can enable depressed people to see themselves in a new setting, and to recover a place of security and belonging within the rich panorama of God's creation, we are helping them. They need to know that they, too, *belong*. It is by enjoying the Creator's handiwork that we often begin to feel again the touch of the Creator's hand.

[11] Thomas Traherne, *The Second Century 76*, in *Centuries* (Mowbray, ed., 1985), p. 91.
[12] Gn. 2:9, RSV.

Divine wisdom – and Job's reaction (Job 40:1–5)

There is a further point to draw from these chapters: they open up a vision of the wisdom of God which transcends any wisdom of humanity. We recall how chapter 28 pointed us in the direction of the divine wisdom. We saw how Elihu, despite his mistakes, also led us the same way. There is a divine wisdom, greater than the wisdom of any human person. God knows things that we do not. He has secrets to which we are not party. There is a pattern to the divine wild order of things of which we could not have dreamed. And here in chapters 38 and 39, the Lord takes Job round with question after question: Did you know this . . . ? Could you comprehend that . . . ? The panorama of God's handiwork is a display of his wisdom, of which Job knows very little.

Then comes a short interchange between the Lord and Job:

> The LORD said to Job:
>
> ²'Will the one who contends with the Almighty correct him?
> Let him who accuses God answer him!'
>
> ³Then Job answered the LORD:
>
> ⁴I am unworthy – how can I reply to you?
> I put my hand over my mouth.
> ⁵I spoke once, but I have no answer –
> twice, but I will say no more.'
>
> (40:1–5)

In this context, Job realizes for the first time that he has in fact overstepped the mark in his protest. He should not have found fault with the Almighty. He should not have insisted on his own understanding. He should not have accused God of injustice. So he replies: 'I am unworthy – how can I reply to you? . . . I will say no more' (40:4). For once, he is practically silenced. God has spoken to Job, and Job has very little left to say

3. The power of God is indicated by the hippo and the crocodile (Job 40:15 – 41:34)

But God has something more to say to Job. In chapters 40 and 41, God seems to be adding to his nature tour some reflections about two of the strangest creatures:

¹⁵'*Look at the behemoth,*
  which I made along with you
  and which feeds on grass like an ox.
¹⁶*What strength he has in his loins,*
  what power in the muscles of his belly!
¹⁷*His tail sways like a cedar;*
  the sinews of his thighs are close-knit.
¹⁸*His bones are tubes of bronze,*
  his limbs like rods of iron.
¹⁹*He ranks first among the works of God,*
  yet his Maker can approach him with his sword.
²⁰*The hills bring him their produce,*
  and all the wild animals play nearby.
²¹*Under the lotus plant he lies,*
  hidden among the reeds in the marsh.
²²*The lotuses conceal him in their shadow;*
  the poplars by the stream surround him.
²³*When the river rages, he is not alarmed;*
  he is secure, though the Jordan should surge against his
    mouth.
²⁴*Can anyone capture him by the eyes,*
  or trap him and pierce his nose?

^{41:1}'*Can you pull in the leviathan with a fishhook*
  or tie down his tongue with a rope?
²*Can you put a cord through his nose*
  or pierce his jaw with a hook?
³*Will he keep begging you for mercy?*
  Will he speak to you with gentle words?
⁴*Will he make an agreement with you*
  for you to take him as your slave for life?
⁵*Can you make a pet of him like a bird*
  or put him on a leash for your girls?
⁶*Will traders barter for him?*
  Will they divide him up among the merchants?
⁷*Can you fill his hide with harpoons*
  or his head with fishing spears?
⁸*If you lay a hand on him,*
  you will remember the struggle and never do it again!
⁹*Any hope of subduing him is false;*
  the mere sight of him is overpowering.
¹⁰*No-one is fierce enough to rouse him.*
  Who then is able to stand against me?
¹¹*Who has a claim against me that I must pay?*

Everything under heaven belongs to me.

¹²*'I will not fail to speak of his limbs,*
his strength and his graceful form.
¹³*Who can strip off his outer coat?*
Who would approach him with a bridle?
¹⁴*Who dares open the doors of his mouth,*
ringed about with his fearsome teeth?
¹⁵*His back has rows of shields*
tightly sealed together;
¹⁶*each is so close to the next*
that no air can pass between.
¹⁷*They are joined fast to one another;*
they cling together and cannot be parted.
¹⁸*His snorting throws out flashes of light;*
his eyes are like the rays of dawn.
¹⁹*Firebrands stream from his mouth;*
sparks of fire shoot out.
²⁰*Smoke pours from his nostrils*
as from a boiling pot over a fire of reeds.
²¹*His breath sets coals ablaze,*
and flames dart from his mouth.
²²*Strength resides in his neck;*
dismay goes before him.
²³*The folds of his flesh are tightly joined;*
they are firm and immovable.
²⁴*His chest is hard as rock,*
hard as a lower millstone.
²⁵*When he rises up, the mighty are terrified;*
they retreat before his thrashing.
²⁶*The sword that reaches him has no effect,*
nor does the spear or the dart or the javelin.
²⁷*Iron he treats like straw*
and bronze like rotten wood.
²⁸*Arrows do not make him flee;*
slingstones are like chaff to him.
²⁹*A club seems to him but a piece of straw;*
he laughs at the rattling of the lance.
³⁰*His undersides are jagged potsherds,*
leaving a trail in the mud like a threshing-sledge.
³¹*He makes the depths churn like a boiling cauldron*
and stirs up the sea like a pot of ointment.
³²*Behind him he leaves a glistening wake;*
one would think the deep had white hair.

33Nothing on earth is his equal –
a creature without fear.
34He looks down on all that are haughty;
he is king over all that are proud.'

The one common factor in all the animals we have met earlier in chapters 38 and 39 is that they are not under human control. God's questioning of Job has shown how much of creation is God's secret, and not open to human power and human competence. We have been given a vision of God's *wisdom*. Now, Behemoth, the hippo (40:15) and Leviathan, the crocodile (41:1), raise the question of God's *power*. God selects two of the creatures which are most feared. These monstrous animals may perhaps be meant here as descriptions of real creatures, or perhaps as a sort of fantasy picture of creatures out of a fable. 'Behemoth' is the plural of the regular Hebrew word for a 'beast', or collectively for 'cattle'. So that this might be a 'plural of magnificence' – Behemoth is the 'beast par excellence'. The Leviathan seems rather like a dragon with flaming breath and smoke from his nostrils. He appears also in Isaiah 27 as a beast of supernatural terror. Taken together, then, Behemoth and Leviathan could stand for the apex of natural and supernatural strength. They embody the inexplicable and the frightening in God's world. Here are two of the mysteries of God. There is a great deal about these two strange creatures which Job does not know and could not control. Here, in your world, Job, are inexplicable, unfathomable and fearful mysteries. Here is a power beyond human power. Before Behemoth and Leviathan, you are powerless. And *yet* both of these are under the control of God. Even the most fearful and monstrous and powerfully terrible things are held within the Creator's hand. 'Everything under heaven belongs to me' (41:11).

This thought was given a Christian context in Abraham Kuyper's famous declaration, 'There is not an inch of this universe of which Jesus Christ does not say "It is Mine".'[13] He was echoing Paul's words in Romans 11: 'From him and through him and to him are all things. To him be the glory for ever and ever.'[14]

He's got the whole wide world – and the little tiny baby – in his hands, says the spiritual. No matter how dark our circumstances, how great our pain, there is no power that can separate us from God. This is spelled out for us at the end of Romans 8 in terms of the love which God shows us in Jesus Christ: 'I am

[13] A. Kuyper, from his Inaugural Lecture in the Free University of Amsterdam.
[14] Rom. 11:36.

convinced that neither death nor life, neither angels nor demons, neither the present nor the future, nor any powers, neither height not depth, nor anything else in all creation, will be able to separate us from the love of God that is in Christ Jesus our Lord.'[15]

What Job was beginning to grasp as the Lord graciously spoke with him has been made clear in full colour in God's revelation of himself in Jesus Christ, his Son. This is the truth of God which can hold on to us whatever our circumstances, in suffering and in joy, in pain and in grief, in life and in death. And the fact is that many people have found it so.

If the nature poems of chapters 38 and 39 speak to us of divine wisdom, Behemoth and Leviathan point us to divine power. But in God's hands, power is not coercive, but always creative. It is the New Testament which fills out the truth that the divine power is the power of love manifest in Jesus.

4. The justice of God means that God alone can vindicate Job (Job 40:6–14)

There is a deeper level still to these chapters, and here we need to turn back to chapter 40:

> [6]*Then the* LORD *spoke to Job out of the storm:*
>
> [7]*'Brace yourself like a man;*
> *I will question you,*
> *and you shall answer me.*
>
> [8]*'Would you discredit my justice?*
> *Would you condemn me to justify yourself?*
> [9]*Do you have an arm like God's,*
> *and can your voice thunder like his?*
> [10]*Then adorn yourself with glory and splendour,*
> *and clothe yourself in honour and majesty.*
> [11]*Unleash the fury of your wrath,*
> *look at every proud man and bring him low,*
> [12]*look at every proud man and humble him,*
> *crush the wicked where they stand.*
> [13]*Bury them all in the dust together;*
> *shroud their faces in the grave.*
> [14]*Then I myself will admit to you*
> *that your own right hand can save you.'*

[15] Rom. 8:38–39.

In many ways, this passage is the centre of the Lord's word to Job.

God is here responding to Job's arguments about theodicy, in which Job complained about the way God governed the world (*cf.* Job 21). All right, says God, *you* rule the world. *You* deck yourself with glory and splendour, *you* clothe yourself with honour and majesty (*cf.* 40:10). *You* pour forth judgments against evil-doers, bring down the proud, hide the wicked in the dust (*cf.* 40:12–13). *You* govern the world in justice, Job, and then I will acknowledge *you*.

This a further response to the question of 40:8: 'Would you discredit my justice?'

The judge who gave the verdict has to see that justice is done. If you are going to pass judgment, Job, can you ensure that justice is carried out? You have insisted on your own vindication, Job, but do *you* have the power to vindicate yourself?

Now we begin to see how the concentration on God's wisdom and power throughout the natural world takes on a further significance. Job must realize that he is no more able to exercise judicial power in the moral realm than he can understand the workings of nature in the natural realm. That is the point of the question in verse 9: 'Do you have an arm like God's, and can your voice thunder like his?' (40:9).

God is reminding Job that he, God, is – despite appearances sometimes – unfailingly just. Here is the book of Job's reply to questions of theodicy.

Wisdom, power and justice

God is a God of wisdom (nature reminds us), of power (the monsters remind us), and of justice (as God now says to Job). With this assertion of divine wisdom, power and justice, we have a description of the character of God in whose hands lie the mysteries of this world's suffering. Before such a God every escape hatch is closed to the human logic which would play one part of God's nature off against another. God is all-knowing, all-powerful *and* all good.

Frequently the problem of suffering is posed in these terms: If God is all-good, it is said, he must wish to abolish all the suffering of which he knows. If he is all-knowing, there is no suffering of which he is unaware. If he is all-powerful, he must be able to do what he wishes. Therefore, because suffering exists in the world, the idea of an omniscient, good and omnipotent God must be incoherent. God cannot be all three: wise and powerful and just. Yet this is precisely what Job is now learning from God. If we say that God is wise and just but not powerful, or wise and powerful but not just, or just and powerful but not wise, our world becomes 'logical' – but it is no longer the world of the living God made known to Job. For Job's God, and ours, is not the end of a logical syllogism – he is a living powerful, wise and just Creator, whose ways are higher than our ways and whose thoughts are higher than our thoughts.[16]

On 23 November 1654, the French philosopher Blaise Pascal had an experience of the 'hidden' God in the person of Jesus Christ. This was a moment of illumination which guided all his future life and work. After his death, a piece of parchment was found sewn into his clothing, recording that experience of Christ. It begins:

> Fire
> 'God of Abraham, God of Isaac, God of Jacob', not of
>   philosophers and scholars.
> Certainty, certainty, heartfelt joy, peace.
> God of Jesus Christ.
> God of Jesus Christ.
> My God and your God. . . .[17]

'God of Abraham . . . not of philosophers and scholars'!

Pascal, like Job, had an experience of the living God who made himself known in personal encounter – not the God who served merely as the end of a philosophical argument.

Divine rationality

We need to be careful here. We are not saying there is no place for the exercise of human reason – Pascal himself was one of the finest minds the world has known. Nor are we saying there is no place for human logic, nor that the ways of God are unreasonable or irrational. God's divine rationality is the basis for all order and rationality in the world. He is the source of our thinking processes, and we are called to worship him with our minds. The book of Job is not inviting us to abandon our reason. It is simply reminding us that through our reason alone we cannot hope to understand the ways of God. The living God is one who is not so much to be debated as encountered, not so much to be discussed as to be known. For the divine rationality is beyond human reason. It cannot be constrained within the canons of human logic. There is a freedom of action in the living God which we cannot always presume to understand. When he makes himself known it is not in terms of logical proof – otherwise all who are capable of following

---

[16] Is. 55:9.   [17] Pascal, *Pensées*, p. 309.

an argument would be bound to believe in him. When God makes himself known it is in gracious personal encounter, which invites a personal response.

This is the sense in which the God of Job is the God of Abraham, and not of the philosophers (like Elihu) or of the scholars (like Bildad). God is wise and powerful and just: he is alive.

A God of surprises

We recall Lesslie Newbigin's concern that our culture is obsessed with the sort of scientific world-view which sees everything in terms of questions which need answering and problems which need solving. The book of Job has shown us that there are questions for which there are no answers this side of heaven, and problems which human logic cannot solve. But it has also shown us the living God – a 'God of surprises' (as Gerard Hughes entitles one of his books),[18] a hidden God who makes his presence known sometimes through his apparent absence, a God whose encounter with us prevents us from tidying up every problem corner of our lives into neat and manageable packages. There is an unhelpful decisiveness in some aspects of Christian faith which gets in the way of meeting God in depth. There is an attempt to have everything buttoned up and secure. There is a defensive need to be sure. The book of Job, instead, brings us face to face with the living God, and invites us to live in his light with all our logical gaps, untidy edges and struggling faith.

In questions of theology, and especially questions about how God orders the world, God has his secrets. Just as we cannot control the hippo, though it is part of God's creation, so we cannot control or even understand some of the deep questions of human suffering. There are some things which have, by their very nature, to be left within the mystery of God.

Job has often insisted that he believes in God's justice, but he has coupled this with an insistence on his own vindication. Here he is now discovering that *God alone has power to vindicate him*. Job cannot take over the running of the universe. This passage in chapter 40 'brings Job to the end of his quest by convincing him that he may and must hand the whole matter over completely to God more trustingly, less fretfully. And do it without insisting that God should first answer all his questions.'[19]

Here, then, we are close to the heart of the book of Job. It stands

---

[18] G. W. Hughes, *God of Surprises* (Darton, Longman & Todd, 1985).
[19] Andersen, p. 287.

as a rebuke to anyone who thinks they could govern the world better than God does.

The story is told of a parson, making his weary way home after a night comforting people during the wartime blitz on London, who met a fellow parson and in his exasperation and bewilderment exclaimed, 'I wish I was on the throne of the universe for ten minutes.' His colleague was not quite as far gone and replied, 'If you were on the throne for ten minutes, I would not wish to live in your world for ten seconds.'

To behave as God suggests in 40:8–14, Job would have to usurp the place of God himself, and become another Satan. As Andersen puts it persuasively:

> Only God can destroy creatively. Only God can transmute evil into good. As Creator, responsible for all that happens in His world, He is able to make everything (good and bad) work together into good. The debate has been elevated to a different level. The reality of God's goodness lies beyond justice. That is why the categories of guilt and punishment [which we kept on meeting in the three friends], true and terrible though they are, can only view human suffering as a consequence of sin, not as an occasion of grace.[20]

Grace

It is in grace that God made himself known to Job. So Job is satisfied. He has not received a direct answer, but he has seen the Lord. He had feared, as many of us do when we are depressed, that though it will turn out all right for others, *we* are the exception. We fear that we have fallen through some hole in the universe, beyond the reach of grace, beyond the world of God, beyond the Creator's control. Job thought he had fallen through a gap in the Creator's management of the world. But now he is reassured. The Creator is holding all things by the word of his power; nothing – not even the silly ostrich or the terrible monsters – are outside his gracious hand. So Job can rest secure, and live with his questions being unanswered. In God, power, justice and wisdom are all aspects of one and the same divine character, so Job can let the matter rest in faith within the mystery of God. Faith, we said, is what God gives us to help us live with uncertainties.

[20] Andersen, p. 288.

5. Job replies (Job 42:1–6)

Then Job replied to the LORD:

> *²'I know that you can do all things;*
> *no plan of yours can be thwarted.*
> *³You asked, "Who is this that obscures my counsel without*
> *knowledge?"*
> *Surely I spoke of things I did not understand,*
> *things too wonderful for me to know.*
>
> *⁴"You said, "Listen now, and I will speak;*
> *I will question you,*
> *and you shall answer me."*
> *⁵My ears had heard of you*
> *but now my eyes have seen you.*
> *⁶Therefore I despise myself*
> *and repent in dust and ashes.'*

Job replies with a statement of humility and submission. 'My ears had heard of you, but now my eyes have seen you' (42:5). His conscience had been quickened, and God's voice has been his teacher. He goes on to say that he now despises what he had said earlier, he has overstepped the mark with his complaints, and for that he humbles himself in contrition and penitence before God.

We must not read this as though Job has at last given in to Zophar's plea that he should repent of his sins. This is not the point. Job has not been overawed by God and humiliated. He has been overwhelmed by the gracious divine presence, and humbly bows his head.

In the New Testament, Simon Peter provides another example. After a fruitless night's fishing, Luke tells us that Jesus called to Simon to put out into the deep water and let out the nets. They caught such a large shoal that their nets broke and the boats became so full that they began to sink. Simon Peter was so overwhelmed with the sense of the divine power displayed before his eyes, and the divine glory shining through the action of Jesus Christ, that he was brought low with a deep realization of his own sinfulness. 'Go away from me, Lord; I am a sinful man!'[21] Job surely feels the same astonishment, and it brings him to a similar sense of his sinfulness, and his need. His penitence, though, is not to suggest any going back on his innocence and integrity. Indeed, God vindicates him directly by saying that he has 'spoken right' (see 42:7–8).

[21] Lk. 5:8.

6. The epilogue (Job 42:7–14)

The poem, which has lasted from the beginning of chapter 3 to 42:6, is over. In 42:7 we revert to prose, rather like the prologue of chapters 1 and 2. There are two features in particular to notice about this epilogue.

First, Job's experience of grace finds expression in his prayer for his friends.

⁷After the LORD had said these things to Job, he said to Eliphaz the Temanite, 'I am angry with you and your two friends, because you have not spoken of me what is right, as my servant Job has. ⁸So now take seven bulls and seven rams and go to my servant Job and sacrifice a burnt offering for yourselves. My servant Job will pray for you, and I will accept his prayer and not deal with you according to your folly. You have not spoken of me what is right, as my servant Job has.' ⁹So Eliphaz the Temanite, Bildad the Shuhite and Zophar the Naamathite did what the LORD told them; and the LORD accepted Job's prayer.

Eliphaz and the others are rebuked by the Lord, for 'you have not spoken of me what is right, as my servant Job has' (42:7). They are told, 'So now take seven bulls and seven rams and go to my servant Job and sacrifice a burnt offering for yourselves. My servant Job will pray for you, and I will accept his prayer and not deal with you according to your folly' (42:8).

Job, the servant of the Lord, offers a prayer on behalf of his friends, by which they are relieved of the wrath of God, and brought to reconciliation with their neighbour. There is a rich vein of theology hidden in these couple of verses! God's anger against the three friends is not his last word. By way of sacrifice and prayer he makes it possible for them to be dealt with graciously. And the sacrifice was made and the prayer offered by the one who was called 'my servant'. This recalls unmistakably the theme we have noticed before from the prophet Isaiah in his Servant Songs[22] and elsewhere. The servant stands in place of the people before God, bringing a sacrifice of atonement, consecration and offering, and praying for God's mercy and grace. Once again, the book of Job is pointing beyond itself to the Mediator between God and human beings, the man Christ Jesus who gave himself as an offering for sins, and now ever lives to make intercession for us.

Many times the book of Job has illustrated themes which come

---

[22] Is. 42:1–4; 49:1–6; 50:4–9; and 52:13 – 53:12.

to clearer focus and richer colour in the life and suffering, death and resurrection of the Lord Jesus. As Peter wrote:

> Christ suffered for you, leaving you an example, that you should follow in his steps.
>
> 'He committed no sin,
> and no deceit was found in his mouth.'
>
> When they hurled their insults at him, he did not retaliate; when he suffered, he made no threats. Instead, he entrusted himself to him who judges justly. He himself bore our sins in his body on the tree, so that we might die to sins and live to righteousness; by his wounds you have been healed.[23]

Secondly, Job's experience of grace is in the here-and-now in this world.

> [10]*After Job had prayed for his friends, the* LORD *made him prosperous again and gave him twice as much as he had before.* [11]*All his brothers and sisters and everyone who had known him before came and ate with him in his house. They comforted and consoled him over all the trouble the* LORD *had brought upon him, and each one gave him a piece of silver and a gold ring.*
> [12]*The* LORD *blessed the latter part of Job's life more than the first. He had fourteen thousand sheep, six thousand camels, a thousand yoke of oxen and a thousand donkeys.* [13]*And he also had seven sons and three daughters.* [14]*The first daughter he named Jemimah, the second Keziah and the third Keren-Happuch.* [15]*Nowhere in all the land were there found women as beautiful as Job's daughters, and their father granted them an inheritance along with their brothers.*
> [16]*After this, Job lived a hundred and forty years; he saw his children and their children to the fourth generation.* [17]*And so he died, old and full of years.*

Why, we may wonder, do we need these paragraphs on the restoration of Job's fortunes? After the gracious gift of God's presence, there is some bathos in this final section. Yet it roots the story firmly in this world. Earlier on, Job's hopes had been centred on some vindication beyond death, in some other world at some other time. But it is here and now, with friends and with the family unit complete again, with restored flocks and herds, that the signs of

[23] 1 Pet. 2:21–24.

God's gracious love are experienced. God's grace is given to the man of faith not in some distant heaven, but here on earth in this life, in which Job is still a pilgrim for some further 140 years. Grace meets us in the felt reality of our human experience. The 'beyond' of God's love meets us here and now.

7. Drawing the threads together

So what remains to be said? We must finally draw some threads together from the whole of our study of this remarkable book.

First, there are more things in heaven and earth than we have ever dreamt of. Job is being caught up into purposes of God of which he knows nothing. There are uncertainties, puzzles and ambiguities in the life of faith which we have to leave within the mystery of God. 'The secret things belong to the LORD.'[24] We must allow God to have his secrets, and receive from him the gift of faith to hold on to him in our uncertainties. Job is above all the Great Believer. May God deepen our faith, even when we are in the dark.

Secondly, there is a warning against inappropriate preaching even of the truth. We saw an insensitivity in the three friends, as they tried to force Job to fit in to their theories, becoming increasingly hardened in their attitudes as he refused to be moulded to their shape. We will never help people if we come to them with predetermined theories and try to squeeze them into our mould. We need rather to learn from the opening scene on the ash heap the ministry of listening, of just being there.

Thirdly, we have seen vividly displayed before our eyes and our emotions, the fact that God's people do suffer. Good and godly people do suffer. Bad things happen to good people. We must learn not to judge a person's spiritual standing according to his or her circumstances and fortunes. We are to beware of the slick equation of blessing from God and life going well. There may be blessings in the pain. There can be a pain that heals, and a closeness to God, even when outer circumstances are all out of line.

In Job's suffering, his body, mind, spirit, relationships, emotions, mind and will were all involved. No part of Job is untouched. All parts are interrelated. We must remember in helping people that we are ministers to the whole person, for we cannot divide people up into separate parts. And the greatest suffering for some people is caused by their faith: the anguish that is felt when God seems to let us down. Yet Job illustrates how moral resolve can grow

[24] Dt. 29:29.

stronger even in adversity. Suffering produces endurance, and endurance character, and character hope.[25]

Fourthly, we recall the difference between a belief in what Pascal called 'the God of the philosophers' and faith in the living God who makes himself known. Again and again the three friends tried to push their understanding of God into a logical corner in which to trap Job. Their understanding of rewards and punishments was distorted through their logic and became simply a belief in the workings of natural causes. Their faith became sterile, linked to a misunderstanding of 'Shaddai', rather than based on the revelation of the living covenant Lord, 'Yahweh'. We are warned by these friends of the need to hold fast to what God has said of himself, and not to be led astray by a twisted logic. We know God only as he has made himself known. For Christian people that is supremely in the revelation of himself in Jesus Christ. In Christ we meet the living God, the God of Abraham, of Isaac and of Jacob – and of Job; not the God of the philosopher.

Fifthly, 'you have heard of Job's perseverance' – so writes James.[26] The Authorized Version uses the phrase 'the patience of Job' which is surely inappropriate! But 'perseverance' (NIV), or 'steadfastness' (RSV) do fit. Here is a man who has listened to the voice of his conscience, and held firm under adversity. The voice of conscience, educated as it needs to be by the Spirit of God (surely that was happening when the Lord questioned Job?) must not be ignored. Just as we do not help others by failing to listen to their needs, so we do not help ourselves by failing to listen to the voice of our conscience.

Sixthly, the law of retribution and a concentration on guilt needs to be set in the broader context of the law of love and a concentration on grace. There is a place for the doctrine of divine judgment, of rewards and punishments, for this is a moral universe. But this doctrine can sometimes be used as a defence against the demands of fellowship, and actually get in the way of the word of grace. Let us see how in the book of Job God himself moves beyond the law of retribution by bestowing on Job the gift of his own gracious presence. Likewise, the doctrine of grace transposes questions of theodicy from a searching for past causes into a hope for future redemption. Job's questions of theodicy are not answered; they are placed in a broader, more personal, context in which they no longer need to be asked.

Seventhly, what matters most from this book is not the preaching or the theology, nor orthodox belief or even Job's own upright

[25] Rom. 5:3–4. [26] Jas. 5:11.

character. Important as all these are, they find their place only in the light of that which is more important than them all, namely walking with God in fellowship with him, to enjoy him in his world. That gift of fellowship can bring profit even out of the greatest suffering. This is what Paul teaches us in 2 Corinthians 12. He was suffering through what he describes as 'a thorn in my flesh, a messenger of Satan, to torment me'.[27] Three times he pleaded with the Lord to take away this affliction. But God replied: 'My grace is sufficient for you, for my power is made perfect in weakness.' 'Therefore,' Paul is able to say, 'I will boast all the more gladly about my weaknesses, so that Christ's power may rest on me . . . when I am weak, then I am strong.'[28]

Finally, from this perspective, we can take heart from the depths of Job's sufferings. Suffering will end: but when, we do not know. But we do know that the Lord will come, and he will transform our 'wounds into worships'.[29] That is the word of hope from Job for people who are waiting with anxiety and uncertainty – wondering, maybe, where God is in their lives. The Lord will come! In the death of Christ, on the cross of Calvary, we are shown the lengths to which God's love will come. And in the cross we see not only the suffering of the crucified God, our Kinsman-Redeemer; we see the gift of new life and hope secured. 'He has borne our griefs and carried our sorrows.'[30]

We are not promised freedom from suffering in this world. 'In the world you will have tribulation.'[31] Nor are we let into all of God's secrets. But we are promised grace. For some, there may be healing and restoration in this life. For others, that gift awaits them in the 'new heavens and the new earth' where there will be no more pain, no more tears, no more death.[32] But for all of us, here and now, there is grace, and there can be hope.

Humble yourselves, therefore, under God's mighty hand, that he may lift you up in due time. Cast all your anxiety on him because he cares for you.

Be self-controlled and alert. Your enemy the devil prowls around like a roaring lion looking for someone to devour. Resist him, standing firm in the faith, because you know that your brothers throughout the world are undergoing the same kind of sufferings.

And the God of all grace, who called you to his eternal glory

[27] 2 Cor. 12:7. [28] 2 Cor. 12:8–10.
[29] Phrase adapted from chapter 39 in Julian of Norwich, *A Revelation of Love*, ed. by M. Glasscoe (Exeter, 1986). [30] Is. 53: 4, RSV.
[31] Jn. 16:33, RSV. [32] Cf. Rev. 21:1–4.

in Christ, after you have suffered a little while, will himself restore you and make you strong, firm and steadfast. To him be the power for ever and ever. Amen.[33]

[33] 1 Pet. 5:6–11.

Appendix

The full biblical text of all the speeches of Eliphaz, Bildad, Zophar and Elihu is printed out in this Appendix.

1. The speeches of Eliphaz

First speech: Job 4 – 5

Eliphaz ventures to speak (4:1–6)

Then Eliphaz the Temanite replied:

> ²*'If someone ventures a word with you, will you be impatient?*
> *but who can keep from speaking?*
> ³*Think how you have instructed many,*
> *how you have strengthened feeble hands.*
> ⁴*Your words have supported those who stumbled;*
> *you have strengthened faltering knees.*
> ⁵*But now trouble comes to you, and you are discouraged;*
> *it strikes you, and you are dismayed.*
> ⁶*Should not your piety be your confidence*
> *and your blameless ways your hope?*

'You reap what you sow' (4:7–11)

> ⁷*'Consider now: Who, being innocent, has ever perished?*
> *Where were the upright ever destroyed?*
> ⁸*As I have observed, those who plough evil*
> *and those who sow trouble reap it.*

APPENDIX

⁹*At the breath of God they are destroyed;*
  at the blast of his anger they perish.
¹⁰*The lions may roar and growl,*
  yet the teeth of the great lions are broken.
¹¹*The lion perishes for lack of prey,*
  and the cubs of the lioness are scattered.

Eliphaz's vision and its meaning (4:12 – 5:7)

¹²*'A word was secretly brought to me,*
  my ears caught a whisper of it.
¹³*Amid disquieting dreams in the night,*
  when deep sleep falls on men,
¹⁴*fear and trembling seized me*
  and made all my bones shake.
¹⁵*A spirit glided past my face,*
  and the hair on my body stood on end.
¹⁶*It stopped,*
  but I could not tell what it was.
 A form stood before my eyes,
  and I heard a hushed voice:
¹⁷*"Can a mortal be more righteous than God?*
  Can a man be more pure than his Maker?
¹⁸*If God places no trust in his servants,*
  if he charges his angels with error,
¹⁹*how much more those who live in houses of clay,*
  whose foundations are in the dust,
  who are crushed more readily than a moth!
²⁰*Between dawn and dusk they are broken to pieces;*
  unnoticed, they perish for ever.
²¹*Are not the cords of their tent pulled up,*
  so that they die without wisdom?"

⁵:¹*'Call if you will, but who will answer you?*
  To which of the holy ones will you turn?
²*Resentment kills a fool,*
  and envy slays the simple.
³*I myself have seen a fool taking root,*
  but suddenly his house was cursed.
⁴*His children are far from safety,*
  crushed in court without a defender.
⁵*The hungry consume his harvest,*
  taking it even from among thorns,
  and the thirsty pant after his wealth.

166

> [6]*For hardship does not spring from the soil,*
> *nor does trouble sprout from the ground.*
> [7]*Yet man is born to trouble*
> *as surely as sparks fly upward.*

Eliphaz extols the goodness of God (5:8–16)

> [8]*'But if it were I, I would appeal to God;*
> *I would lay my cause before him.*
> [9]*He performs wonders that cannot be fathomed,*
> *miracles that cannot be counted.*
> [10]*He bestows rain on the earth;*
> *he sends water upon the countryside.*
> [11]*The lowly he sets on high,*
> *and those who mourn are lifted to safety.*
> [12]*He thwarts the plans of the crafty,*
> *so that their hands achieve no success.*
> [13]*He catches the wise in their craftiness,*
> *and the schemes of the wily are swept away.*
> [14]*Darkness comes upon them in the daytime;*
> *at noon they grope as in the night.*
> [15]*He saves the needy from the sword in their mouth;*
> *he saves them from the clutches of the powerful.*
> [16]*So the poor have hope,*
> *and injustice shuts its mouth.*

The happiness of the person who responds to suffering in the right spirit (5:17–27)

> [17]*'Blessed is the man whom God corrects;*
> *so do not despise the discipline of the Almighty.*
> [18]*For he wounds, but he also binds up;*
> *he injures, but his hands also heal.*
> [19]*From six calamities he will rescue you;*
> *in seven no harm will befall you.*
> [20]*In famine he will ransom you from death,*
> *and in battle from the stroke of the sword.*
> [21]*You will be protected from the lash of the tongue,*
> *and need not fear when destruction comes.*
> [22]*You will laugh at destruction and famine,*
> *and need not fear the beasts of the earth.*
> [23]*For you will have a covenant with the stones of the field,*
> *and the wild animals will be at peace with you.*

²⁴*You will know that your tent is secure;*
  you will take stock of your property and find nothing
    missing.
²⁵*You will know that your children will be many,*
  and your descendants like the grass of the earth.
²⁶*You will come to the grave in full vigour,*
  like sheaves gathered in season.

²⁷*'We have examined this, and it is true.*
  So hear it and apply it to yourself.'

Second speech: Job 15

Eliphaz rebukes Job for his irreverence (15:1–6)

Then Eliphaz the Temanite replied:

²*'Would a wise man answer with empty notions*
  or fill his belly with the hot east wind?
³*Would he argue with useless words,*
  with speeches that have no value?
⁴*But you even undermine piety*
  and hinder devotion to God.
⁵*Your sin prompts your mouth;*
  you adopt the tongue of the crafty.
⁶*Your own mouth condemns you, not mine;*
  your own lips testify against you.

Who does Job think he is? (15:7–16)

⁷*'Are you the first man ever born?*
  Were you brought forth before the hills?
⁸*Do you listen in on God's council?*
  Do you limit wisdom to yourself?
⁹*What do you know that we do not know?*
  What insights do you have that we do not have?
¹⁰*The grey-haired and the aged are on our side,*
  men even older than your father.
¹¹*Are God's consolations not enough for you,*
  words spoken gently to you?
¹²*Why has your heart carried you away,*
  and why do your eyes flash,
¹³*so that you vent your rage against God*
  and pour out such words from your mouth?

¹⁴*"What is man, that he could be pure,*
or one born of woman, that he could be righteous?
¹⁵*If God places no trust in his holy ones,*
if even the heavens are not pure in his eyes,
¹⁶*how much less man, who is vile and corrupt,*
who drinks up evil like water!

The traditional picture of the evil-doer (15:17–35)

¹⁷*'Listen to me and I will explain to you;*
let me tell you what I have seen,
¹⁸*what wise men have declared,*
hiding nothing received from their fathers
¹⁹*(to whom alone the land was given*
when no alien passed among them):
²⁰*All his days the wicked man suffers torment,*
the ruthless through all the years stored up for him.
²¹*Terrifying sounds fill his ears;*
when all seems well, marauders attack him.
²²*He despairs of escaping the darkness;*
he is marked for the sword.
²³*He wanders about – food for vultures;*
he knows the day of darkness is at hand.
²⁴*Distress and anguish fill him with terror;*
they overwhelm him, like a king poised to attack,
²⁵*because he shakes his fist at God*
and vaunts himself against the Almighty,
²⁶*defiantly charging against him*
with a thick, strong shield.

²⁷*'Though his face is covered with fat*
and his waist bulges with flesh,
²⁸*he will inhabit ruined towns*
and houses where no-one lives,
houses crumbling to rubble.
²⁹*He will no longer be rich and his wealth will not endure,*
nor will his possessions spread over the land.
³⁰*He will not escape the darkness;*
in flame will wither his shoots,
and the breath of God's mouth will carry him away.
³¹*Let him not deceive himself by trusting what is worthless,*
for he will get nothing in return.
³²*Before his time he will be paid in full,*
and his branches will not flourish.

³³*He will be like a vine stripped of its unripe grapes,*
  like an olive tree shedding its blossoms.
³⁴*For the company of the godless will be barren,*
  and fire will consume the tents of those who love bribes.
³⁵*They conceive trouble and give birth to evil;*
  their womb fashions deceit.'

Third speech: Job 22

Eliphaz says God is not really concerned with Job (22:1–4)

Then Eliphaz the Temanite replied:

²*'Can a man be of benefit to God?*
  Can even a wise man benefit him?
³*What pleasure would it give the Almighty if you were*
  righteous?
  What would he gain if your ways were blameless?
⁴*Is it for your piety that he rebukes you*
  and brings charges against you?

This must prove Job's wickedness (22:5–11)

⁵*'Is not your wickedness great?*
  Are not your sins endless?
⁶*You demanded security from your brothers for no reason;*
  you stripped men of their clothing, leaving them naked.
⁷*You gave no water to the weary*
  and you withheld food from the hungry,
⁸*though you were a powerful man, owning land –*
  an honoured man, living on it.
⁹*And you sent widows away empty-handed*
  and broke the strength of the fatherless.
¹⁰*That is why snares are all around you,*
  why sudden peril terrifies you,
¹¹*why it is so dark and you cannot see,*
  and why a flood of water covers you.

Eliphaz thinks Job must believe God is unconcerned (22:12–20)

¹²*'Is not God in the heights of heaven?*
  And see how lofty are the highest stars!
¹³*Yet you say, "What does God know?*
  Does he judge through such darkness?

¹⁴*Thick clouds veil him, so he does not see us*
   as he goes about in the vaulted heavens."
¹⁵*Will you keep to the old path*
   that evil men have trod?
¹⁶*They were carried off before their time,*
   their foundations washed away by a flood.
¹⁷*They said to God, "Leave us alone!*
   What can the Almighty do to us?"'
¹⁸*Yet it was he who filled their houses with good things,*
   so I stand aloof from the counsel of the wicked.

¹⁹*'The righteous see their ruin and rejoice;*
   the innocent mock them, saying,
²⁰*"Surely our foes are destroyed,*
   and fire devours their wealth."

**Eliphaz appeals to Job to agree with God and be at peace
(22:21–30)**

²¹*'Submit to God and be at peace with him;*
   in this way prosperity will come to you.
²²*Accept instruction from his mouth*
   and lay up his words in your heart.
²³*If you return to the Almighty, you will be restored:*
   If you remove wickedness far from your tent
²⁴*and assign your nuggets to the dust,*
   your gold of Ophir to the rocks in the ravines,
²⁵*then the Almighty will be your gold,*
   the choicest silver for you.
²⁶*Surely then you will find delight in the Almighty*
   and will lift up your face to God.
²⁷*You will pray to him, and he will hear you,*
   and you will fulfil your vows.
²⁸*What you decide on will be done,*
   and light will shine on your ways.
²⁹*When men are brought low and you say, "Lift them up!"*
   then he will save the downcast.
³⁰*He will deliver even one who is not innocent,*
   who will be delivered through the cleanness of your
      hands.'

2. The speeches of Bildad

First speech: Job 8

Bildad affirms the justice of God (8:1–7)

Then Bildad the Shuhite replied:

> [2]*'How long will you say such things?*
> *Your words are a blustering wind.*
> [3]*Does God pervert justice?*
> *Does the Almighty pervert what is right?*
> [4]*When your children sinned against him,*
> *he gave them over to the penalty of their sin.*
> [5]*But if you will look to God*
> *and plead with the Almighty,*
> [6]*if you are pure and upright,*
> *even now he will rouse himself on your behalf*
> *and restore you to your rightful place.*
> [7]*Your beginnings will seem humble,*
> *so prosperous will your future be.*

Bildad appeals to ancient wisdom (8:8–22)

> [8]*'Ask the former generations*
> *and find out what their fathers learned,*
> [9]*for we were born only yesterday and know nothing,*
> *and our days on earth are but a shadow.*
> [10]*Will they not instruct you and tell you?*
> *Will they not bring forth words from their*
> *understanding?*
> [11]*Can papyrus grow tall where there is no marsh?*
> *Can reeds thrive without water?*
> [12]*While still growing and uncut,*
> *they wither more quickly than grass.*
> [13]*Such is the destiny of all who forget God;*
> *so perishes the hope of the godless.*
> [14]*What he trusts in is fragile;*
> *what he relies on is a spider's web.*
> [15]*He leans on his web, but it gives way;*
> *he clings to it, but it does not hold.*
> [16]*He is like a well-watered plant in the sunshine,*
> *spreading its shoots over the garden;*
> [17]*it entwines its roots around a pile of rocks*

    and looks for a place among the stones.
¹⁸*But when it is torn from its spot,*
    that place disowns it and says, "I never saw you."
¹⁹*Surely its life withers away,*
    and from the soil other plants grow.

²⁰*'Surely God does not reject a blameless man*
    or strengthen the hands of evildoers.
²¹*He will yet fill your mouth with laughter*
    and your lips with shouts of joy.
²²*Your enemies will be clothed in shame,*
    and the tents of the wicked will be no more.'

Second speech: Job 18

How long will Job go on like this? (18:1–4)

Then Bildad the Shuhite replied:

²*'When will you end these speeches?*
    Be sensible, and then we can talk.
³*Why are we regarded as cattle*
    and considered stupid in your sight?
⁴*You who tear yourself to pieces in your anger,*
    is the earth to be abandoned for your sake?
    Or must the rocks be moved from their place?

Bildad portrays the fate of the wicked (18:5–21)

⁵*'The lamp of the wicked is snuffed out;*
    the flame of his fire stops burning.
⁶*The light in his tent becomes dark;*
    the lamp beside him goes out.
⁷*The vigour of his step is weakened;*
    his own schemes throw him down.
⁸*His feet thrust him into a net*
    and he wanders into its mesh.
⁹*A trap seizes him by the heel;*
    a snare holds him fast.
¹⁰*A noose is hidden for him on the ground;*
    a trap lies in his path.
¹¹*Terrors startle him on every side*
    and dog his every step.
¹²*Calamity is hungry for him;*
    disaster is ready for him when he falls.

¹³*It eats away parts of his skin;*
death's firstborn devours his limbs.
¹⁴*He is torn from the security of his tent*
and marched off to the king of terrors.
¹⁵*Fire resides in his tent;*
burning sulphur is scattered over his dwelling.
¹⁶*His roots dry up below*
and his branches wither above.
¹⁷*The memory of him perishes from the earth;*
he has no name in the land.
¹⁸*He is driven from light into darkness*
and is banished from the world.
¹⁹*He has no offspring or descendants among his people,*
no survivor where once he lived.
²⁰*Men of the west are appalled at his fate;*
men of the east are seized with horror.
²¹*Surely such is the dwelling of an evil man;*
such is the place of one who knows not God.'

Third speech: Job 25

How can a person be righteous before this God? (25:1–6)

Then Bildad the Shuhite replied:

²*'Dominion and awe belong to God;*
he establishes order in the heights of heaven.
³*Can his forces be numbered?*
Upon whom does his light not rise?
⁴*How then can a man be righteous before God?*
How can one born of woman be pure?
⁵*If even the moon is not bright*
and the stars are not pure in his eyes,
⁶*how much less man, who is but a maggot –*
a son of man, who is only a worm!'

A possible further speech: Job 26:5–14

⁵*'The dead are in deep anguish,*
those beneath the waters and all that live in them.
⁶*Death is naked before God;*
Destruction lies uncovered.
⁷*He spreads out the northern skies over empty space;*
he suspends the earth over nothing.

⁸*He wraps up the waters in his clouds,*
yet the clouds do not burst under their weight.
⁹*He covers the face of the full moon,*
spreading his clouds over it.
¹⁰*He marks out the horizon on the face of the waters*
for a boundary between light and darkness.
¹¹*The pillars of the heavens quake,*
aghast at his rebuke.
¹²*By his power he churned up the sea;*
by his wisdom he cut Rahab to pieces.
¹³*By his breath the skies became fair;*
his hand pierced the gliding serpent.
¹⁴*And these are but the outer fringe of his works;*
how faint the whisper we hear of him!
Who then can understand the thunder of his power?'

3. The speeches of Zophar

First speech: Job 11

Zophar rebukes Job and calls on God to speak (11:1–6)

Then Zophar the Naamathite replied:

²*'Are all these words to go unanswered?*
Is this talker to be vindicated?
³*Will your idle talk reduce men to silence?*
Will no-one rebuke you when you mock?
⁴*You say to God, "My beliefs are flawless*
and I am pure in your sight."
⁵*Oh, how I wish that God would speak,*
that he would open his lips against you
⁶*and disclose to you the secrets of wisdom,*
for true wisdom has two sides.
Know this: God has even forgotten some of your sin.

Zophar extols God's wisdom (11:7–12)

⁷*'Can you fathom the mysteries of God?*
Can you probe the limits of the Almighty?
⁸*They are higher than the heavens – what can you do?*
They are deeper than the depths of the grave – what can
you know?

APPENDIX

⁹*Their measure is longer than the earth*
and wider than the sea.

¹⁰*'If he comes along and confines you in prison*
and convenes a court, who can oppose him?
¹¹*Surely he recognises deceitful men;*
and when he sees evil, does he not take note?
¹²*But a witless man can no more become wise*
than a wild donkey's colt can be born a man.

Zophar sets out the way of repentance and the blessings of the penitent (11:13–20)

¹³*'Yet if you devote your heart to him*
and stretch out your hands to him,
¹⁴*if you put away the sin that is in your hand*
and allow no evil to dwell in your tent,
¹⁵*then you will lift up your face without shame;*
you will stand firm and without fear.
¹⁶*You will surely forget your trouble,*
recalling it only as waters gone by.
¹⁷*Life will be brighter than noonday,*
and darkness will become like morning.
¹⁸*You will be secure, because there is hope;*
you will look about you and take your rest in safety.
¹⁹*You will lie down, with no-one to make you afraid,*
and many will court your favour.
²⁰*But the eyes of the wicked will fail,*
and escape will elude them;
their hope will become a dying gasp.'

Second speech: Job 20

Zophar's impatience (20:1–3)

Then Zophar the Naamathite replied:

²*'My troubled thoughts prompt me to answer*
because I am greatly disturbed.
³*I hear a rebuke that dishonours me,*
and my understanding inspires me to reply.

Zophar describes the fate of the wicked (20:4–11)

⁴*'Surely you know how it has been from of old,*
ever since man was placed on the earth,

⁵*that the mirth of the wicked is brief,*
  the joy of the godless lasts but a moment.
⁶*Though his pride reaches to the heavens*
  and his head touches the clouds,
⁷*he will perish for ever, like his own dung;*
  those who have seen him will say, "Where is he?"
⁸*Like a dream he flies away, no more to be found,*
  banished like a vision of the night.
⁹*The eye that saw him will not see him again;*
  his place will look on him no more.
¹⁰*His children must make amends to the poor;*
  his own hands must give back his wealth.
¹¹*The youthful vigour that fills his bones*
  will lie with him in the dust.

'Sin brings its rewards' (20:12–22)

¹²*'Though evil is sweet in his mouth*
  and he hides it under his tongue,
¹³*though he cannot bear to let it go*
  and keeps it in his mouth,
¹⁴*yet his food will turn sour in his stomach;*
  it will become the venom of serpents within him.
¹⁵*He will spit out the riches he swallowed;*
  God will make his stomach vomit them up.
¹⁶*He will suck the poison of serpents;*
  the fangs of an adder will kill him.
¹⁷*He will not enjoy the streams,*
  the rivers flowing with honey and cream.
¹⁸*What he toiled for he must give back uneaten;*
  he will not enjoy the profit from his trading.
¹⁹*For he has oppressed the poor and left them destitute;*
  he has seized houses he did not build.

²⁰*'Surely he will have no respite from his craving;*
  he cannot save himself by his treasure.
²¹*Nothing is left for him to devour;*
  his prosperity will not endure.
²²*In the midst of his plenty, distress will overtake him;*
  the full force of misery will come upon him.

Zophar speaks of God's fierce anger (20:23–29)

²³*'When he has filled his belly,*

God will vent his burning anger against him
and rain down his blows upon him.
²⁴Though he flees from an iron weapon,
a bronze-tipped arrow pierces him.
²⁵He pulls it out of his back,
the gleaming point out of his liver.
Terrors will come over him,
²⁶   total darkness lies in wait for his treasures.
A fire unfanned will consume him
and devour what is left in his tent.
²⁷The heavens will expose his guilt;
the earth will rise up against him.
²⁸A flood will carry off his house,
rushing waters on the day of God's wrath.
²⁹Such is the fate God allots the wicked,
the heritage appointed for them by God.'

Possible third speech

More on the fate of the wicked (27:13–23)

¹³'Here is the fate God allots to the wicked,
the heritage a ruthless man receives from the Almighty;
¹⁴However many his children, their fate is the sword;
his offspring will never have enough to eat.
¹⁵The plague will bury those who survive him,
and their widows will not weep for them.
¹⁶Though he heaps up silver like dust
and clothes like piles of clay,
¹⁷what he lays up the righteous will wear,
and the innocent will divide his silver.
¹⁸The house he builds is like a moth's cocoon,
like a hut made by a watchman.
¹⁹He lies down wealthy, but will do so no more;
when he opens his eyes, all is gone.
²⁰Terrors overtake him like a flood;
a tempest snatches him away in the night.
²¹The east wind carries him off, and he is gone;
it sweeps him out of his place.
²²It hurls itself against him without mercy
as he flees headlong from its power.
²³It claps its hands in derision
and hisses him out of his place.'

4. The speeches of Elihu

First speech: Job 32 – 33

Introduction to Elihu (32:1–5)

*So these three men stopped answering Job, because he was righteous
in his own eyes. ²But Elihu son of Barakel the Buzite, of the family
of Ram, became very angry with Job for justifying himself rather
than God. ³He was also angry with the three friends, because they
had found no way to refute Job, and yet had condemned him. ⁴Now
Elihu had waited before speaking to Job because they were older
than he. ⁵But when he saw that the three men had nothing more
to say, his anger was aroused.*

Elihu's reason for intervening (32:6–22)

So Elihu son of Barakel the Buzite said:

⁶'I am young in years,
  and you are old;
that is why I was fearful,
  not daring to tell you what I know.
⁷I thought, "Age should speak;
  advanced years should teach wisdom."
⁸But it is the spirit in a man,
  the breath of the Almighty, that gives him
    understanding.
⁹It is not only the old who are wise,
  not only the aged who understand what is right.

¹⁰'Therefore I say: Listen to me;
  I too will tell you what I know.
¹¹I waited while you spoke,
  I listened to your reasoning;
while you were searching for words,
¹² I gave you my full attention.
But not one of you has proved Job wrong;
  none of you has answered his arguments.
¹³Do not say, "We have found wisdom;
  let God refute him, not man."
¹⁴But Job has not marshalled his words against me,
  and I will not answer him with your arguments.*

¹⁵*'They are dismayed and have no more to say;*
  words have failed them.
¹⁶*Must I wait, now that they are silent,*
  now that they stand there with no reply?
¹⁷*I too will have my say;*
  I too will tell what I know.
¹⁸*For I am full of words,*
  and the spirit within me compels me;
¹⁹*inside I am like bottled-up wine,*
  like new wineskins ready to burst.
²⁰*I must speak and find relief;*
  I must open my lips and reply.
²¹*I will show partiality to no-one,*
  nor will I flatter any man;
²²*for if I were skilled in flattery,*
  my Maker would soon take me away.

Elihu's case against Job (33:1–33)

'But now, Job, listen to my words;
  pay attention to everything I say.
²*I am about to open my mouth;*
  my words are on the tip of my tongue.
³*My words come from an upright heart;*
  my lips sincerely speak what I know.
⁴*The Spirit of God has made me;*
  the breath of the Almighty gives me life
⁵*Answer me then, if you can;*
  prepare yourself and confront me.
⁶*I am just like you before God;*
  I too have been taken from clay.
⁷*No fear of me should alarm you,*
  nor should my hand be heavy upon you

⁸*'But you have said in my hearing –*
  I heard the very words –
⁹*"I am pure and without sin;*
  I am clean and free from guilt.
¹⁰*Yet God has found fault with me;*
  he considers me his enemy.
¹¹*He fastens my feet in shackles;*
  he keeps close watch on all my paths."

¹²*'But I tell you, in this you are not right,*

for God is greater than man.
¹³*Why do you complain to him*
that he answers none of man's words?
¹⁴*For God does speak – now one way, now another –*
though man may not perceive it.
¹⁵*In a dream, in a vision of the night,*
when deep sleep falls on men
as they slumber in their beds,
¹⁶*he may speak in their ears*
and terrify them with warnings,
¹⁷*to turn man from wrongdoing*
and keep him from pride,
¹⁸*to preserve his soul from the pit,*
his life from perishing by the sword.
¹⁹*Or a man may be chastened on a bed of pain*
with constant distress in his bones,
²⁰*so that his very being finds food repulsive*
and his soul loathes the choicest meal.
²¹*His flesh wastes away to nothing,*
and his bones, once hidden, now stick out.
²²*His soul draws near to the pit,*
and his life to the messengers of death.

²³*'Yet if there is an angel on his side*
as a mediator, one out of a thousand,
to tell a man what is right for him,
²⁴*to be gracious to him and say,*
"Spare him from going down to the pit;
I have found a ransom for him" –
²⁵*then his flesh is renewed like a child's;*
it is restored as in the days of his youth.
²⁶*He prays to God and finds favour with him,*
he sees God's face and shouts for joy;
he is restored by God to his righteous state.
²⁷*Then he comes to men and says,*
"I have sinned, and perverted what was right,
but I did not get what I deserved.
²⁸*He redeemed my soul from going down to the pit,*
and I shall live to enjoy the light."

²⁹*'God does all these things to a man –*
twice, even three times –
³⁰*to turn back his soul from the pit,*
that the light of life may shine on him.

³¹'*Pay attention, Job, and listen to me;*
   be silent, and I will speak.
³²*If you have anything to say, answer me;*
   speak up, for I want you to be cleared.
³³*But if not, then listen to me;*
   be silent, and I will teach you wisdom.'

Second speech: Job 34

Elihu says Job is in the wrong before God (34:1–9)

Then Elihu said:

²'*Hear my words, you wise men;*
   listen to me, you men of learning.
³*For the ear tests words*
   as the tongue tastes food.
⁴*Let us discern for ourselves what is right;*
   let us learn together what is good.

⁵'*Job says, "I am innocent,*
   but God denies me justice.
⁶*Although I am right,*
   I am considered a liar;
although I am guiltless,
   his arrow inflicts an incurable wound."
⁷*What man is like Job,*
   who drinks scorn like water?
⁸*He deeps company with evildoers;*
   he associates with wicked men.
⁹*For he says, "It profits a man nothing*
   when he tries to please God."

Elihu defends God's justice (34:10–30)

¹⁰'*So listen to me, you men of understanding.*
   Far be it from God to do evil,
   from the Almighty to do wrong.
¹¹*He repays a man for what he has done;*
   he brings upon him what his conduct deserves.
¹²*It is unthinkable that God would do wrong,*
   that the Almighty would pervert justice.
¹³*Who appointed him over the earth?*
   Who put him in charge of the whole world?

¹⁴If it were his intention
    and he withdrew his spirit and breath,
¹⁵all mankind would perish together
    and man would return to the dust.

¹⁶'If you have understanding, hear this;
    listen to what I say.
¹⁷Can he who hates justice govern?
    Will you condemn the just and mighty One?
¹⁸Is he not the One who says to kings, "You are worthless,"
    and to nobles, "You are wicked,"
¹⁹who shows no partiality to princes
    and does not favour the rich over the poor,
    for they are all the work of his hands?
²⁰They die in an instant, in the middle of the night;
    the people are shaken and they pass away;
    the mighty are removed without human hand.

²¹'His eyes are on the ways of men;
    he sees their every step.
²²There is no dark place, no deep shadow,
    where evildoers can hide.
²³God has no need to examine men further,
    that they should come before him for judgment.
²⁴Without enquiry he shatters the mighty
    and sets up others in their place.
²⁵Because he takes note of their deeds,
    he overthrows them in the night and they are crushed.
²⁶He punishes them for their wickedness
    where everyone can see them,
²⁷because they turned from following him
    and had no regard for any of his ways.
²⁸They caused the cry of the poor to come before him,
    so that he heard the cry of the needy.
²⁹But if he remains silent, who can condemn him?
    If he hides his face, who can see him?
    Yet he is over man and nation alike,
³⁰   to keep a godless man from ruling,
    from laying snares for the people.

Elihu exposes Job's foolishness (34:31–37)

³¹'Suppose a man says to God,
    "I am guilty but will offend no more.

³²*Teach me what I cannot see;*
    if I have done wrong, I will not do so again."
³³*Should God then reward you on your terms,*
    when you refuse to repent?
  You must decide, not I;
    so tell me what you know.

³⁴*'Men of understanding declare,*
    wise men who hear me say to me,
³⁵*"Job speaks without knowledge;*
    his words lack insight."
³⁶*Oh, that Job might be tested to the utmost*
    for answering like a wicked man!
³⁷*To his sin he adds rebellion;*
    scornfully he claps his hands among us
    and multiplies his words against God.'

Third speech: Job 35

Elihu argues that God is distant and detached (35:1–16)

Then Elihu said:

²*'Do you think this is just?*
    You say, "I shall be cleared by God."
³*Yet you ask him, "What profit is it to me,*
    and what do I gain by not sinning?"

⁴*'I would like to reply to you*
    and to your friends with you.
⁵*Look up at the heavens and see;*
    gaze at the clouds so high above you.
⁶*If you sin, how does that affect him?*
    If your sins are many, what does that do to him?
⁷*If you are righteous, what do you give to him,*
    or what does he receive from your hand?
⁸*Your wickedness affects only a man like yourself,*
    and your righteousness only the sons of men.

⁹*'Men cry out under a load of oppression;*
    they plead for relief from the arm of the powerful.
¹⁰*But no-one says, "Where is God my Maker,*
    who gives songs in the night,
¹¹*who teaches more to us than to the beasts of the earth*
    and makes us wiser than the birds of the air?"

¹²*He does not answer when men cry out*
because of the arrogance of the wicked.
¹³*Indeed, God does not listen to their empty plea;*
the Almighty pays no attention to it.
¹⁴*How much less, then, will he listen*
when you say that you do not see him,
that your case is before him
and you must wait for him,
¹⁵*and further, that his anger never punishes*
and he does not take the least notice of wickedness
¹⁶*So Job opens his mouth with empty talk,*
without knowledge he multiplies words.'

Fourth speech: Job 36 – 37

The purpose of suffering (36:1–15)

Elihu continued:

²*'Bear with me a little longer and I will show you*
that there is more to be said on God's behalf.
³*I get my knowledge from afar;*
I will ascribe justice to my Maker.
⁴*Be assured that my words are not false;*
one perfect in knowledge is with you.

⁵*'God is mighty, but does not despise men;*
he is mighty, and firm in his purpose.
⁶*He does not keep the wicked alive*
but gives the afflicted their rights.
⁷*He does not take his eyes off the righteous;*
he enthrones them with kings
and exalts them for ever.
⁸*But if men are bound in chains,*
held fast by cords of affliction,
⁹*he tells them what they have done –*
that they have sinned arrogantly.
¹⁰*He makes them listen to correction*
and commands them to repent of their evil.
¹¹*If they obey and serve him,*
they will spend the rest of their days in prosperity
and their years in contentment.
¹²*But if they do not listen,*
they will perish by the sword
and die without knowledge.

13'*The godless in heart harbour resentment;*
  even when he fetters them, they do not cry for help.
14*They die in their youth,*
  among male prostitutes of the shrines.
15*But those who suffer he delivers in their suffering;*
  he speaks to them in their affliction.

This is applied to Job (36:16–25)

16'*He is wooing you from the jaws of distress*
  to a spacious place free from restriction,
  to the comfort of your table laden with choice food.
17*But now you are laden with the judgment due to the*
    wicked;
  judgment and justice have taken hold of you.
18*Be careful that no-one entices you by riches;*
  do not let a large bribe turn you aside.
19*Would your wealth*
  or even all your mighty efforts
  sustain you so you would not be in distress?
20*Do not long for the night,*
  to drag people away from their homes.
21*Beware of turning to evil,*
  which you seem to prefer to affliction.

22'*God is exalted in his power.*
  Who is a teacher like him?
23*Who has prescribed his ways for him*
  or said to him, "You have done wrong"?
24*Remember to extol his work,*
  which men have praised in song.
25*All mankind has seen it;*
  men gaze on it from afar.

God in nature, his power in the storm (36:26 – 37:13)

26'*How great is God – beyond our understanding!*
  The number of his years is past finding out.
27*He draws up the drops of water,*
  which distil as rain to the streams;
28*the clouds pour down their moisture*
  and abundant showers fall on mankind.
29*Who can understand how he spreads out the clouds,*
  how he thunders from his pavilion?

³⁰*See how he scatters his lightning about him,*
    bathing the depths of the sea.
³¹*This is the way he governs the nations*
    and provides food in abundance.
³²*He fills his hands with lightning*
    and commands it to strike its mark.
³³*His thunder announces the coming storm;*
    even the cattle make known its approach.

^{37:1}*'At this my heart pounds*
    and leaps from its place.
²*Listen! Listen to the roar of his voice,*
    to the rumbling that comes from his mouth.
³*He unleashes his lightning beneath the whole heaven*
    and sends it to the ends of the earth.
⁴*After that comes the sound of his roar;*
    he thunders with his majestic voice.
    When his voice resounds,
    he holds nothing back.
⁵*God's voice thunders in marvellous ways;*
    he does great things beyond our understanding.
⁶*He says to the snow, "Fall on the earth,"*
    and to the rain shower, "Be a mighty downpour."
⁷*So that all men he has made may know his work,*
    he stops every man from his labour.
⁸*The animals take cover;*
    they remain in their dens.
⁹*The tempest comes out from its chamber,*
    the cold from the driving winds.
¹⁰*The breath of God produces ice,*
    and the broad waters become frozen.
¹¹*He loads the clouds with moisture;*
    he scatters his lightning through them.
¹²*At his direction they swirl around*
    over the face of the whole earth
    to do whatever he commands them.
¹³*He brings the clouds to punish men,*
    or to water his earth and show his love.

The Almighty is exalted in power: fear him (37:14–24)

¹⁴*'Listen to this, Job;*
    stop and consider God's wonders.

¹⁵*Do you know how God controls the clouds*
and makes his lightning flash?
¹⁶*Do you know how the clouds hang poised,*
those wonders of him who is perfect in knowledge?
¹⁷*You who swelter in your clothes*
when the land lies hushed under the south wind,
¹⁸*can you join him in spreading out the skies,*
hard as a mirror of cast bronze?

¹⁹*'Tell us what we should say to him;*
we cannot draw up our case because of our darkness.
²⁰*Should he be told that I want to speak?*
Would any man ask to be swallowed up?
²¹*Now no-one can look at the sun,*
bright as it is in the skies
after the wind has swept them clean.
²²*Out of the north he comes in golden splendour;*
God comes in awesome majesty.
²³*The Almighty is beyond our reach and exalted in power;*
in his justice and great righteousness, he does not oppress.
²⁴*Therefore, men revere him,*
for does he not have regard for all the wise in heart?'